What! And Give Up Show Business?

Jim —
Seen any good movies
lately?
Ask Anderson. She'll
know of three!

Best.

Peter Wooley
Dec '01

What!
And Give Up
Show Business?

*A View from
the Hollywood Trenches*

Peter Wooley

FITHIAN PRESS, SANTA BARBARA, CALIFORNIA, 2001

Cover photo by Kevyn Major Howard

Published by Fithian Press
A division of Daniel and Daniel, Publishers, Inc.
Post Office Box 1525
Santa Barbara, CA 93102
www.danielpublishing.com

LIBRARY OF CONGRESS CATALOGING-IN-PUBLICATION DATA
Wooley, Peter, (date)
    What! and give up show business? : a view from the Hollywood trenches /
by Peter Wooley.
        p.   cm
    ISBN 1-56474-366-7 (pbk : alk. paper)
    1. Wooley, Peter, (date)   2. Motion picture art directors—United States—
Biography.   I. Title.
    PN1998.3.W67 A3 2001
    791.43'025'092—dc21   00-011057

For Linda,
for everything

Most people look at everything and see
nothing. We look at nothing and see
everything.

—*P.W.*

The past is what you remember, imagine
you remember, convince yourself you
remember, or pretend you remember.

—*Harold Pinter*

Contents!

Acknowledgments

I wish to thank all those good folks, both living and dead, whose antics inspired me to "go ahead and write it." I would like to thank my mother, June Wooley, for not putting me in a burlap bag and tossing me into the Ohio River when she had the chance. Bless Linda for not putting a steak knife in my heart while I slept. To my daughter, Stephanie, who made the first editorial pass and got the chapters in intelligent order, and my son, Christopher, who kept me from beating my IMac to death with my 5-iron, and who designed the cover, I am eternally indebted. And thanks to Crayton Smith, my agent for over thirty years, who always saw to it that I didn't work for nothing, and always kept my ass in leather. Finally, I wish a special thank-you to my editor, Eric Larson, who taught me the value of the common comma.

Art Department

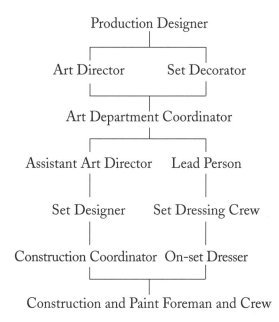

Production Designer

Art Director   Set Decorator

Art Department Coordinator

Assistant Art Director   Lead Person

Set Designer   Set Dressing Crew

Construction Coordinator   On-set Dresser

Construction and Paint Foreman and Crew

Production designer: Head of the art department on a film or television project. Duties consist of working closely with the director to create a "look" for the picture. The production designer picks locations, designs sets, and oversees set construction and decoration, and also maintains a close working relationship with the writer, director of photography, set decorator, construction coordinator, property master, wardrobe designer, and their crews, and, when necessary, the producer.

What! And Give Up Show Business?

Call Time

THIRTY-FOUR THOUSAND FEET. First class, of course. If I'm going to die, I might as well have my ass in leather. I'm returning from yet another movie-making adventure. After thirty-seven years of doing whatever it is I do, I guess I should count myself lucky to still look on the whole process as an adventure.

Consider this: I get a script, read it, say yes, get on an airplane, and travel to someplace I have never been before. I am met by someone I don't know, who takes me to a strange place to live. He introduces me to sixty to eighty strangers who have read the same script. We have a lot of meetings, and we discuss how much time and money we have to create a work of art, *the motion picture.* Hopefully, but not necessarily, we are all speaking the same language. After three to six months and some millions of dollars, we will finish. Whereupon I will say goodbye to sixty to eighty of my closest friends, climb on an airplane, and put my ass in leather. An adventure.

I design movies and television movies. I also do the occasional pilot, and have even done some television series, but mostly I have settled into movies and movies of the week. I read a script, have long talks with the producer and director, scout locations, and decide what this movie is going to look like. Of course the writer's words guide me, but sometimes time and money, or even art, will demand that some changes be made. If I had to write a job description of what it is I do it would say, "I am responsible for everything you see on the screen except the actors, God forbid." I prefer to think of my job as translating words into pictures. It sounds more poetic. I also see my job as being part-time psychiatrist, wet nurse, animal trainer, spiritual adviser, soothsayer, bullshit artist, Viking, shepherd, and hit man. Those sixty to eighty other people all have their specific jobs to do. Theirs are just as important as mine.

And then there is the fear. There is the fear of failing, the fear of not knowing what you're doing, and the fear of being thought of as the fool. It takes a special kind of person to survive this business. Not better, God knows, just special.

I was born in East Liverpool, Ohio, when the world was in black and white. I met and fell in love with a skinny blond with hair halfway down her back. We were in church kindergarten at the time, and even though I had not yet discovered testosterone I knew that someday I would and I wanted to be prepared. Some years later, that skinny little blond had the bad taste to marry me, and that was some forty-odd years ago.

I studied architecture only to discover that it wasn't any fun. Somehow or other I had gotten it into my head that whatever I was going to do with my life, I should have fun doing it. We were living in Southern California at the time, and I was trying to support a wife and two children as an architect.

I met Tracy Bousman, who, because of a writers' strike in the movie business, was staying alive working in the same architectural office as I was. He told me stories of working in the movie business, and it struck some sort of demented chord in the deep recesses of my psyche.

One night, lying in bed staring at the ceiling, I announced to the skinny little blond with hair halfway down her back (hereinafter referred to as Linda) that I was not a happy camper. "What's

*I was born in East Liverpool, Ohio, when the
world was in black and white. (Summer 1943.)*

the problem, you big stud?" she asked. She often speaks this way, I
suspect, out of wishful thinking.

"The movie business," I answered. "I want to get into the
movie business."

Five seconds passed, and she said, "Go for it." We were
twenty-nine years old, with a new house in Orange County, two
children, and my business doing pretty well, and this dummy says,
"Go for it." That's like giving Lizzy Borden and ax and saying,
"Have fun, dear."

The next day I called Warner Brothers, because I liked their
cartoons. Obviously I didn't know where to start, but luck was my
copilot. I got the head of the art department on the phone and he
gave me an interview. Seems my timing was pretty good; they
needed draftsmen and, boy, was I a draftsman. I went to work at
Warners for $3.50 an hour and never looked back. The world, at
that time, was still in black and white, sometimes.

Enough about me. Let me tell you more about Linda. I really

I guess she sort of liked me too.
(Summer 1952.)

fell in love with her when I was in the seventh grade and she was in the sixth. By that time, I had discovered testosterone. Her father was the proprietor of Lane's Grocery Store, across the street from McKinley School. She worked in the store in the evenings, and always gave me the biggest five-cent ice cream cones you ever saw. I guess she sort of liked me too. I hung out in front of the store in the evenings, and I spent my time looking in the window at her and setting off the fire alarm on the lamp post out front. We have been pretty much together since then. When I graduated a year before her, I went into the navy. When she graduated a year later, her father sold the store and used the money to stake her to a year at the Pasadena Playhouse. She then moved to New York to pursue a singing career. She got an agent and began singing in clubs on the east coast. Linda worked at the Copa in New York, the 500 Club in Atlantic City, the Bradford Roof in Boston, and the Downbeat in Montreal, among other places. In the meantime I did my time for Uncle Sam, then went back to East Liverpool and went to work for an architect.

Linda got a gig at the now-defunct Dunes in Las Vegas, and we were miserable not being together. I showed up in Vegas as she was about to finish her two-week engagement. We boarded a plane for Los Angeles, got an apartment in Hollywood, and got married in a cemetery. We were married at Forest Lawn at the Church of the Recessional, a Celtic chapel that a few weeks before had played host to Clark Gable's funeral. We spent a year in Los Angeles. I was the assistant commandant at St. John's Military Academy, and Linda was a housewife and mommy of our first-born, Stephanie.

"Ladies and gentlemen, the lovely and, indeed, the very talented Miss Linda Lane."

We moved back to Ohio, and I went to Kent State University and studied architecture. Linda went to work singing me through school. She worked some nice places and some toilets in and around Cleveland and Pittsburgh. We still laugh at how many times she was introduced the same way: "Ladies and gentlemen, the lovely and, indeed, the very talented Miss Linda Lane." She was also with the resident company of the Kenley Players, a summer stock theater group in Warren, Ohio. During all of this we made another baby, Christopher. When I left Kent State we went back to Los Angeles, and Linda went back to being a housewife. As my success in the movie business grew and the children became more maintenance free, Linda started to sing again. She began to work what we called the Smokehouse Circuit. She was working nights, and I was working days, and that wasn't working at all.

Linda has always been an independent lady, and she always wanted to have what she called her "own money." Now, who can argue with that? She started her own company, which is involved in the consumer electronic business. It is much too complicated to explain except to say that now that I'm retiring, she is making a bloody fortune, and I am the luckiest son of a bitch in the world. Did I mention that she is drop-dead beautiful? She still sets off my fire alarm.

Linda threw a surprise sixtieth birthday party for me at the Half Moon Saloon in Big Sky, Montana. My mother chose that momentous occasion to lay a piece of information on me that explained just how "special" I really am: I was, she announced, conceived in the rumble seat of a Model "A" Ford in the parking lot of a nightclub in Pennsylvania! I haven't been able to thank her enough for that information. That single fact alone, I feel, qualifies me as "special," which makes me more than eligible for a position in show business. Forget that crap about being born in a trunk in the Princess Theater in Pocatello, Idaho. I was in show business at my conception! Thanks, Ma, for making me special.

Truth be told, despite all my wanderings, I'm happiest at home and hearth with hugs and kisses from wife, children, and, God bless everyone, grandchildren. If there is real and true magic in the world, grandchildren produce it. In the movies, magic is all smoke and mirrors. I know, because I make the smoke and hold the mirrors.

Speaking of Big Sky, Montana, we have a place there. Not a ranch or even a log cabin, but a one-bedroom condo loft by the fifth tee box of an Arnold Palmer-designed golf course. In the winter a family of moose lives back there. We have been going up to Big Sky for about twenty years now for the best skiing in the world in the winter, and fishing, riding, golfing, and being silly in the summer, spring, and fall. The most refreshing thing I can think of to do between pictures is go up there and hang with the locals. Unlike the denizens of this velvet sewer known as Los Angeles, the good folks in Montana do not have any hidden agendas. They are who they appear to be when you first meet them and they don't "rightly have a good reason to change." When I go there I have no adjustments to make with my friends. It's very soothing to be in Big Sky, Montana, after dodging the emotional traffic of Hollywood.

These, then, are the musings and ramblings of my career in Lotusland. I present them from 'another point of view than the usual Hollywood remembrances. I'm no star or major player, just a working guy who doesn't see this as the glamorous business of "show" that all those other rarified people have presented in their so-called memoirs. This is a view from the trenches. It is a view rarely written about because publishers don't see it as interesting or noteworthy. However, when I relate these stories to people, always they say, "You should write that down." Here goes.

Going Home To Do
Going Home

*Experience is the worst teacher. It gives the
test before presenting the lesson.*

—Vernon Law

MY FIRST FEATURE as a production designer was an epic
for MGM called *Going Home*. I got on the picture late and left it
a little early but I put my stamp on it nonetheless. It was filmed in
and around Pittsburgh, which is forty miles from my hometown,
East Liverpool, Ohio. This, of course, gave me the opportunity to
go home on the occasional weekend and show off. If I didn't know
before, I found out then what a real waste of time is.

One evening I went into the Dandee Bar, my old haunt in
East Liverpool. I sat down next to an old classmate, and we started
to talk as if I had been there every night for the previous ten years.
"So, where are you living these days?"

"Out in Los Angeles." I don't want to clutter up the conversation with too many details.

"I got a friend out there. Maybe you know him...."

"Los Angeles is a rather large place chock full of people. I
doubt I would know him."

"Don't be too sure. He's a crazy bastard. We were in the Army
together. He was quite a cut-up. Used to piss on the sergeant's leg
when the sergeant was washing his hair in the shower. That damn
sergeant never knew he was doing it." He told me the guy's name,

and of course I didn't know him. Now every time I take a shower I try to keep my eyes open, just in case his friend shows up.

"So, you livin' back here now?" My mother saw to it that no matter what I was doing in Hollywood the local paper was informed, and the local paper informed East Liverpool. I was the only person from there ever to get my name on the screen, so I was something of a local celebrity, I thought.

"Actually, no, I'm working on a project up in Pittsburgh." I was still trying to keep it simple.

"Pittsburgh, huh? I been meaning to go there, but I gotta get my oil changed." That conversation changed the way I saw myself. It was a map, of sorts, of the pitfalls of being a well-traveled, educated, and erudite human in a sea of assholes.

The picture starred Robert Mitchum, and a large portion of the filming was done in a recently shut-down prison known as the Allegheny County Workhouse and Inebriate Asylum. No, I'm not lying. It was a spooky Gothic red-brick old place long past its prime. Ghosts were constantly pulling at your sleeve, and a single sound seemed to echo forever. What made it even spookier was that it appeared the prisoners were still there. The tin plates were set out in the mess hall waiting, it seemed, for the next meal. Papers covered the guards' desks as though the guards would be sitting back down any minute. There was a tailor shop where they wove material and sewed it into prisoners' uniforms. Looms were stopped with material in them, and sewing machines, silent with half a shirt or part of a pair of jeans, sat waiting.

I kept snooping around and found a Jolly Green Giant suit. It was great, made of individual green corduroy leaves lined with gray prison shirt material. It was an off-the-shoulder number complete with matching hat. Even better, it fit me, so I removed my clothes and put it on to give my construction and set dressing crew a thrill. I don't think it thrilled them all that much, but it sure as hell made them laugh. News of me in the giant suit swept the company like a flu bug.

I was leaving the picture a few days early to go to Louisiana to do *Sounder*, so the set decorator, Audrey Blaisdell, asked to take me to a goodbye dinner. "Come down to my room around seven-thirty. We'll have a drink, and I'll buy dinner."

When Blaisdell opened her door she was dressed in an Army general's uniform. Over her shoulder I saw my head painter, Tom "Black Bart" Bartholomew (no relation to *Blazing Saddles* Black Bart), dressed as a duck, and the property master, Ernie Sawyer, who was just about as wide as he was tall, dressed in a skin-tight Batman outfit. Without a word, I turned and ran back to my room, undressed, put on my Jolly Green Giant suit, and returned to Blaisdell's. We had a drink, then another, and when we could stand the hilarity no longer, we decided to go down to the best restaurant in the hotel. In our costumes.

The restaurant had a salad bar, and Sawyer and I were doing our stand-up routine near the radishes. A local came over to us and said, "Hey, you guys been in a parade or something?"

I said in my best Green Giant voice, "Hell, buddy, my whole life is a parade!" The management asked us, much more nicely than we deserved, to please find another restaurant for our hilarity, so we left to a smattering of applause.

The company was shooting at night in downtown McKeesport in a car lot that we had turned into a trailer park. It just didn't seem fair not to share these outfits with them, so off we went. There were about two thousand locals behind police lines watching the shooting, and we managed to get the car through the mess and pulled in right behind the camera. They were shooting a very serious scene. Robert Mitchum, holding a bag of groceries, was in a phone booth talking to his son (Jan Michael Vincent), who had just attempted to rape Mitchum's fiancée, played by Brenda Vacarro.

Out of the car we got: a general, a duck, the Jolly Green Giant, and Batman. Mitchum saw us first, about the same time as the crowd. Out of the phone booth flew a bag of groceries, followed by Mitchum, who was near hysterics. Over the crowd noise he yelled to me, "Just think, somewhere in this city there is probably a gay ex-convict your size."

I tell this story for a reason. It is extremely difficult to make a movie. There are constant trials and problems that keep the angst level on high most of the time. I think it is important to do things to keep it as light as possible. We have to keep reminding ourselves that it is not nuclear war we are taking part in, just a movie.

One afternoon, Mitchum and I were sitting in the hotel bar having a drink. It was the middle of the afternoon, and we were the only people in the joint. Can you imagine how it feels to be a snot-nosed kid from East Liverpool sitting in a bar having a beer with Robert Mitchum? He had been my hero since I saw him at the American Theater in downtown East Liverpool playing Pigiron in the movie *Gung Ho*. At the entrance to the bar I noticed two teenage girls frantically trying to get together pencil and paper so they could come over to get Mitchum's autograph. Over they came, and looking up at Mitchum with adoring eyes they squeaked, "Mr. Mitchum, could we please have your autograph?" He was very sweet. He asked their names and wrote them over his signature. The girls looked adoringly at their treasures. Then one of the girls turned her attention to me. All the love went out of her face and voice as she said to me, "Are you anybody?"

"My mother thinks so," I volunteered. Mitchum fell off the barstool.

Way Down South in the Land of Sugar Cane

A desk is a dangerous place from which to watch the world.

—*John Le Carre*

WHEN I LEFT PITTSBURGH I flew directly to Baton Rouge, Louisiana, to start *Sounder*. So long to home and hearth for the next four months. I was not the production designer of record on *Sounder*. That honor went to my dear and now dead friend Walter Scott Herndon. He had gotten the script and was so impressed with it that he brought it over to my house for me to read. I loved it as he did, and told him that I would work on it under any position we could work out with the producer, Robert Radnitz. It was to be directed by the brash and gentle Martin Ritt. So when *Sounder* started, there was no time for me to go home.

Sounder was a Newberry Award-winning book written by William H. Armstrong. Lonni Elder III took on the chore of adapting it to the screen. Set in the mid-1930s, it is the story of a black sharecropping family, the Morgans. The father (Paul Winfield) is accused of stealing a ham to feed his family and is sent to prison. The story then focuses on the oldest son (Kevin Hicks), who is still a preteen, and his attempt to keep the family going. The film was shot in the summer of 1971, and we shot it in Clinton, Louisiana, near Baton Rouge. We couldn't shoot it in Georgia, where the book was set. Seems we couldn't find a hotel in

Georgia where we could house the black cast along with the predominantly white crew. Well, well, well.

The production was financed by the Mattel toy company. It had a very modest budget, but Robert Radnitz had given us a little more time to prepare it than was usual. Even today I marvel at how much we were able to do with the money we had, simply because we had more time to be creative. There is a lesson there for the filmmakers of the future, and it has gone completely unnoticed to this day.

Herndon and I decided to "double-team" it. That is, he would be responsible for half of the sets, and I would take on the rest. We would help each other when help was needed, and of course he would have the final word, and he attend all the dreaded meetings. It was to be the first and only time in my career that I could just go out and play and not have to go through those "I don't know, what do you think?" meetings.

Herndon and I shared a common vision for the film. We knew we had something special, and we were determined to treat it gently and with respect. We found the perfect location for the Morgan house on the property of a gentleman I will call J.B., who also owned a sawmill on the same property. J.B. was probably the richest guy in town yet he was a pleasant, self-made man with little or no pretensions. His wife, on the other hand, was something else.

About a week before we started to shoot, I was invited to dinner at J.B.'s. At the head of the table was J.B. with his wife to his left and me on the right. The rest of the family was on down the table, as the black maid served. Idiot that I am, I got us into a discussion on the "black thing." It heated up right away, and I couldn't or didn't want to get it stopped. Our first assistant director was an African-American. I said to J.B.'s wife, "What would you say if he was having dinner here right now?"

Without taking her eyes from mine, she slowly and deliberately reached across the table and moved my water glass out of the way. She then tapped on the center of my dinner plate with a polished fingernail and said, "A nigger will never sit where you're sitting." I put my napkin down, got up, and left.

As I was walking home from J.B.'s, I got to thinking about the repercussions of this little dinner encounter. What if he threw us off his property? It could set production back as much as two months, and put me in the position to "never work in this town or any other town again." Never mind that what she said was morally reprehensible, I started it. "To hell with it," I thought as I went to bed. I had done what I thought was right. I could always go back to architecture.

J.B. had what they call a "camp" out on the Amite River. It was a pretty good-size house trailer sitting on a much larger concrete pad, all covered by a large tin roof. No women allowed. J.B. would have all-men parties out there about every other week, with manly food and manly drink. Since I was now considered a "local" I was always invited, and always attended these something less than black-tie soirees. Most of the "made" men in town attended, including the Fish and Game officers, as well as the local sheriff. Just a bunch of good ol' boys eatin' catfish and drinkin' bourbon and white lightning. Hell, I became master of ceremonies.

The next morning, as I was walking out to the set and pondering my future out of show business, J.B. headed me off with his pick-up. Suddenly there we were, nose to nose, he still sitting in the truck. But he had the biggest smile on his face I had ever seen on him. "Comin' out to the camp tonight?"

I was stunned but what the hell, I might as well keep up the charade. "What are you having to eat, you old fart?" I queried. Right below the level of the truck window he was holding a plastic bag, which he raised and placed in front of my nose.

"Bulls' balls," he laughed and drove away. I went out to the camp that night and ate those damn bulls' balls and washed them down with bourbon, and we never spoke again of the incident at dinner. It is probably not a good idea to call on me to give advice on race relations.

With our construction budget we couldn't afford to build a proper farm for the Morgan family. Instead I found the perfect house about twenty miles away from the site in a swamp. It was abandoned, overgrown with vines, and infested with wasps, rats, and snakes. The construction guys got a bulldozer and cleared the vines away. Industrial-strength bug bombs got rid of the wasps, and we worked around the rats and snakes. We cut the house into pieces as big as we could carry, put it on the back of a flat-bed truck, and hauled it to our site. We built a solid floor to hold cameras, lights, and crew, and set the house on top of it. We were able to orient it to the sun and we knew what the camera would see through the windows. In the next parish, Walter found a pole shed to put behind the house. Each pole was numbered, and it was taken down and reassembled. A pole shed, by the way, is a small elevated storage barn.

Abraham Lincoln was just about the last guy in America who could split rails, it seemed, but finally I found a local guy who was willing to give it a try. For pay, he wanted a goat. We bought him a goat. We found out later that he wanted it to barbecue, but, what the hell, that's his business. Now we had a proper fence to put around the farm to keep the mule in place. The mule. Gotta get a mule. Joe Stemley, an affable black farmer who lived right down the road, rented us his mule. It was a good mule, able to pull a plow for the filming and apparently comfortable around a lot of people. It was also capable of doing its "mule thing" around the barnyard. That is, it ate and left the right kind of set dressing around the yard. The only problem we had was that it would get out at night and run off into the nearby woods. I would put a notice in the paper offering a fifteen-dollar reward for the return of the mule, and someone would always return it. I soon discovered that people were coming out at night and stealing the mule for the reward, but the way I figured it, fifteen dollars was a cheap price to pay for good community relations. We realized we had to feed the mule, so Joe Stemley came to the rescue again. He sold me a small cornfield. We picked the corn, put it in the pole shed, and fed the damn mule.

The other thing we had to build at the farm was a chimney on the house, for we had been unable to move the original brick chimney from the swamp. I found a respected bricklayer in the black community, told him to leave his tools at home, pretend he was a farmer, and come over and build us a crooked chimney. He scratched his head, walked in circles, and finally agreed to build our chimney, but only if we promised never to tell who did it.

We built the farm beside a small pond. It was picturesque and practical. Herndon and I even went out on a Sunday and planted a vegetable garden in front of the house so the Morgans would have some vegetables. The crew ate them all during shooting.

One of the opening shots of the picture was an early-morning establishing shot of the farm. Everyone agreed that the best shot was across the small pond, with the house reflected in it. John Alonzo, the cinematographer, asked, "Is there anything you can do to make the pond darker?" A reasonable request, since the darker the pond the better the reflection. On my next outing at J.B.'s camp I put the problem to the Fish and Game guys over a tumbler of bourbon. They said we could broadcast straw across the pond, and as it settled to the bottom it would take all the offending little particles of dirt suspended in the water to the bottom, leaving the water clear and, therefore, darker. The only problem was that the straw would heat up the water and cause all the fish to die. Bad idea. We persisted, and found a harmless chemical that would polarize the particles, causing them to join together into clumps of dirt and sink to the bottom. No dead fish, but clear water. *Voilà*, a perfect reflection.

By far the most creative contribution we made to the film was the sugarcane mill. One day Walter was riding around with our local liaison, Paul Littlefield, when he noticed what he thought was a pot-bellied stove in the middle of a field. "What's that out there?"

"That's a cane mill," answered Littlefield. "They're not used very much anymore. People take their sugar cane to a commercial outfit to process it into cane syrup nowadays. It's a pretty labor-intensive job using one of those things. You have to put a long lodge pole on top of that thing and attach a mule to the end of it. The mule walks in circles while you hand feed cane into one side of it. Juice comes out the other side. Then you put that juice in a big flat galvanized pan with a fire under it, and tend it until…."

Walter knew he was on to something. In the book the family grew corn. After it was harvested, they took it to a scale, had it weighed, gave most of it to "the man," and got to keep the rest as their pay.

Good for a book, but not so great visually for a film. It bothered Herndon and me, but until then we hadn't been able to come up with anything better.

We called back to Hollywood and told them about our find. The family would grow sugar cane, harvest it, and make cane syrup. The father, who returned from prison with a bad leg, would have a tough time operating the mill, making the oldest boy just as important in running things as he had been when Daddy was away. We were geniuses!

The problem, of course, was that no one actually knew how to make cane syrup. Paul Littlefield found an ancient black man who still lived in a house that looked very much like the one we had created. He once had been a sharecropper and had lived in that house all his life. When he got too old to work, the people who owned the land just let him stay and they took care of him. He was the area's last remaining authority on the back yard making of cane syrup.

I was assigned to go out to his place for instructions. My first visit was like a ray of sunshine. Or should I say moonshine? He was a delightful old gentleman who laughed a lot and told great stories. We sat on the front porch in the evening light, he in his rocker and me on the floor with my back against a post that held up the porch roof. We passed a Mason jar of white lightning back and forth, and he beguiled me with stories of the Old South while he taught me to make cane syrup. It took four evenings of instruction and white lightning for me to learn all I needed to know. Now that I think back, I wish he had also taught me how to make that great moonshine.

Sugar cane! We needed sugar cane! We not only needed sugar cane for the cane mill sequences, we needed to grow a few acres for the family to tend. They were scheduling the picture to be shot in sequence, which is rare in filmmaking for a number of reasons. It is not uncommon to shoot the last scenes first, but this particular picture lent itself to being shot in sequence. This was a plus for us, because we could actually show the crops and garden growing. Even though we had a lot of time, however, we didn't have time to grow three acres of sugar cane and harvest it. Good old Joe Stemley came to the rescue yet again and provided us with the harvested sugar cane for the cane mill sequences, but the growing cane was another problem.

I went to the Farmers' Co-op in Clinton for some advice. "What do you have that looks like sugar cane and grows like a son of a bitch?" I asked, feeling like a stupid city jerk, which I was. They got out their catalogs and started to talk among themselves. I stood there feeling more and more like a jerk. After a lot of yelling and arguing among themselves, they turned their attention back to me. Now I was starting to feel like a stupid insecure city jerk.

"Here it is, boy, the answer to your dreams. It's a hybrid millet. Looks like sugar cane and grows like a son of a bitch."

"How fast is your son of a bitch?" I asked.

"Thursday," was the reply.

"Thursday," I screamed, "what the hell does that mean?"

"If you plant it today, it will be out of the ground on Thursday."

What the hell, I didn't have any better solution, so I bought the seed, had the three acres of ground plowed and planted, and prayed. Every morning I went into the field and looked at it and said, "Grow, you son of a bitch." On Wednesday the field looked like it did the day we planted. Wednesday night Herndon and I went to the only saloon in town and toasted the gods of hybrid millet.

Thursday morning we went to the field together—for moral support, I suppose—and as we approached the field, we saw a distinct green patina across the whole three acres. In fact, the millet was out of the ground about three inches, and damned if it didn't look like sugar cane. Later, as the shooting progressed, that millet grew to the exact height required.

My "office hours" were generally from three o'clock to five

o'clock every day. My "office" was Herman's Country Club. Herman's was a one-room wooden structure that sat cheek by jowl with the railroad tracks. It was dwarfed by huge stacks of pulpwood waiting for trains to take them to paper mills all over the country. Inside, along the left wall, was a long wooden bench. The wall behind it was covered with political posters dating back to Huey Long. On the right was a plain counter from which Herman conducted business. Next to the counter was a series of soft-drink coolers. They were the old-fashioned kind, and they contained broken, dirty ice and beer and soft drinks. Behind the counter and running the length of the room were shelves of liquor. There was a small serving window in the front so that Herman could serve the blacks. No sense in not getting their money, even if you didn't allow them inside, I guess. From three to five o'clock every white man in Clinton made an appearance at Herman's, however. Here's the way it worked: You went inside and ordered a drink. Herman would give you a quart of whatever you ordered. You paid for it, he handed you a marking pen, and you wrote your name on the label. You picked up a plastic cup, opened one of the coolers, and filled your cup with dirty ice. You poured yourself a drink, and left the bottle on the counter. When you left, Herman would put your bottle on the shelf. Next day when you walked in, he would place it back down on the counter in front of you. The sheriff, Mr. Arch (locals pronounced it "Mistatch"), would be there with his drink, as would the city fathers, businessmen, field hands, farmers, and a few trustees from the county jail. It was not uncommon to have fifty men in there drinking and talking.

There was a back door leading out to an outhouse that was really close to the train tracks. You tried not to be in there when a non-stop train came flashing by. That could turn a pleasant few minutes into a near-death experience.

I always needed something to keep the production moving. Sometimes it would be a road scraper, sometime it would be something as strange as unlabeled canned goods. Or local extras. Whatever I needed, I would put out the word in Herman's. It wouldn't take long for someone to come up to me and say, "Mista

Pete, I unnerstand ya'll are lookin' for some ol' telephone poles. I got some out to my place just takin' up space."

I would say, "Hell, yes, what is that you're drinkin' there? Herman, give this gentleman a bottle of whatever it is he's drinkin'." Those office hours saved the company thousands of dollars.

Sounder was a unique learning experience for me, the likes of which I have never had since. It was so early in my career that it was like getting a Ph.D., not just in filmmaking, but in farming, economics, general social studies, and the attitudes of the Old South as well.

Cleopatra Jones
Meets Black Bart

*When I used to read fairytales, I fancied
that kind of thing never happened, and
now here I am in the middle of one.*
                              —Lewis Caroll

I WAS DOING A BLACK exploitation picture for Warner
Brothers called *Cleopatra Jones,* starring a six-foot-tall actress
named Tamara Dobson. Even by Hollywood standards, the director was way, way "out there." His brain lived in a place normal
people would never go. When I worked with him I lived there too.
His name was Jack Starrett. I say "was" because he is no longer
with us. Like a meteor, he streaked through our skies. We looked
up in wonder and watched him hit the denser air and become
brighter and brighter until we had to shield our eyes from the bril-
liance and the beauty of it all. Then he was no more. We became
friends during the shooting, and I grabbed that meteor's tail and
held on for dear life.

One day about halfway through filming I mentioned to
Starrett that the following day we were going to be shooting a set
on the stage, and it would be a good idea if he would come by after we wrapped today so that we could look at it together. He had
not seen it, and I thought he should see what he was getting into.
To ensure his arrival, I told him I would have vast quantities of
Jack Daniel's on hand to ward off evil spirits and ease the pain of

37

looking up all day at a six-foot actress who couldn't act. The set was the apartment of a pimp and drug dealer, and it was "pimp-lavish," complete with fish tanks. I backed my MG Midget onto the stage and turned up the radio to give the set the proper ambiance, and Cheryl Kearney, the set decorator, got us some ice with which to tame Mr. Daniel. Starrett and I checked the set, then turned our attention to the gentleman in the bottle.

Some hours later, when we were in the middle of a discussion of either quantum physics or breasts—I can't remember which—the stage phone rang. It was nine-thirty at night, and I should have known better than to answer it. Little did I know how much that call would affect my career. It was Ed Morey, the head of production, calling for me. "Hey, glad I caught you. Mel Brooks wants to see you right away in his office. Warners have recommended you to him to design *Black Bart*. Get your ass over there."

Now, a sane or sober person would have said, "Tell him you couldn't find me. I need time to prepare for a meeting like that. Set it up for first thing in the morning." Being neither sane nor sober, I simply said, "Okay." I told Starrett to sit tight, I would be back in a few minutes to take him home, and I staggered across the lot.

The legendary Mel Brooks had come out west to do his first "Hollywood" movie, *Black Bart*, after his phenomenal successes in *The Producers*, shot in New York, and *The Twelve Chairs*, shot in Europe. Everyone in town knew about the picture, an irreverent look at Hollywood's depiction of westerns, blacks, and Native Americans. The name would be changed after shooting ended to *Blazing Saddles* just in time for Frankie Laine to record the title song.

By now a parade of production designers had marched through Brooks's office hoping for the coveted position. I was currently working on the second film of my career, and figured I had about as much chance as that snowball in that place. The last thing Starrett said to me as I left the stage was, "If you get the movie, you have to get me the part of Gabby Johnson." Yes, Jack was also a very good actor, as well as a fair saloon singer.

"Sure, Jack, I'll tell my old buddy Mel to be sure to pencil you in." I continued my uneven walk to destiny.

When I walked into Brooks's office, trying to look sober, there was the man himself sitting with his producer, Michael Hertzberg, and his production manager, Bill Owens. After introductions Brooks said, "Sit down," and Hertzberg added, "Yeah, pull up a floor and sit down." It was at this precise moment that I thought I knew what Hollywood was all about. I sat on the floor. I simply collapsed my legs and allowed my drunken ass to hit the floor. My first thought in the nanosecond this took was, "You'll never work in this town again." To make matters worse, because of the size of Brooks's desk I completely lost eye contact with him. He stood up, leaned over his desk, grinned down at me and said, "Well, I'll be a son of a bitch."

I know enough about comedy to never walk away from a joke. Once it's out there, live with it. I knew better than to get up off the floor. I leaned slightly to the side and rested against the couch, forcing Brooks to remain standing during the whole meeting, which fortunately, didn't last long.

"Have you ever done a western?" Brooks asked, trying, I'm sure, to put some dignity back into the proceedings. I had not, but I knew he hadn't either, so I answered with a question.

"Have you?" He didn't answer, but he continued to stand and grin. I took this as a good sign. The script was sitting on his desk, and he slid it across the vast playing surface. It soared into the air and plopped on my lap. "Here, take this home, read it, and give me one good and funny visual idea." Meeting over. Well, there went that career.

Well, I was in this far; I might as well carry out the charade. I read the script, and as everyone knows it was a trailblazing hoot. There is a scene in which, after her musical number, Lili von Shtupp invites Black Bart into her dressing room. After slipping into "something more comfortable" Lili turns out the lights and in voice-over says, "Tell me, schatzi, is it twue vat zey say about the way you people are gifted?" We hear the sound of a zipper. After a

long pause, she continues, "Oh, oh, it's twue, it's twue, it's twue...."
In the original script there was one more line to end the scene.
Happily for Warner Brothers and good-taste mongers everywhere
the line was cut from the film.

I, however, chose to make this my "one good and funny visual
idea." I drew a Panavision-size rectangle, painted it totally black,
and wrote beneath it that one never-to-be-heard line, "Excuse me,
ma'am, you're sucking my arm." I figured, and rightly so, that since
I wasn't going to be working in this town again, I might as well go
out with a flourish.

A few days later I screwed up my courage and, sober, went in
with my sketch to face the man. He looked at it and laughed. Hell,
what else was he supposed to do? I beat a sensible retreat and went
back to my office to begin packing. Later I was told that after I
left, Brooks waved the sketch in the air and said, "How can I *not*
hire this little son of a bitch?"

As I walked into my office the phone was ringing. It was
Brooks. "Listen, kid, you're on the team. You're number 25, and
wear your lifts." Since neither Brooks nor I even approached the
altitude of Tamara Dobson, I said, "I will if you will," and hung up
on him.

And, of course, I did the picture.

Jack Starrett, in the meantime, was bugging me about getting
an interview with Brooks to play the part of Gabby Johnson. The
character was modeled after the old western character actor Gabby
Hayes. Although much younger than Hayes, Starrett already had
the famous beard and, besides, he did the most dead-on impression of the original anyone had ever seen. So I set up a meeting.
When Jack walked into the office, Brooks took one look at him
and said, "You're too tall and too young." At that Starrett spun 360
degrees, and when he faced Brooks again, he had lost six inches in
height and aged twenty years. "Now, hold on there, Sidewinder,"
roared Jack. Mel fell out of his chair, and Jack got the part.

As I look back on all of this, it comes to me that this story is
really what Hollywood is all about. Or at least what it's supposed
to be about.

"Have you ever done a western?" Brooks asked. "Have you?" I replied.
That's Brooks in the leather jacket and me on his
left—being "bad guys."

I would like to set the record straight on one other thing.
Mongo, played with brilliant economy by Alex Karras, did not actually hit that horse. The nag was trained to "take" a punch, like
any stuntman is trained. Seems you can train a horse to fall to the
left or the right, much like a politician. The shot you see in the
film is actually take two. On take one, Karras was standing too far
back from the horse because he was afraid he would really hit it,
and the shot didn't look real. When Brooks explained to him that
the horse would fall down like any stuntman, Karras stepped up
and let it fly. The next time you see that shot, look at the way the
horse falls. You can train a horse to fall, but you can't train a horse
to fall in the same direction as his head. Horses are too smart for
that. Notice that his head swings to the left from a right-hand
punch, but his body falls to the right.

My mother came to visit while we were shooting, and my
wife, Linda, brought her onto the back lot. I think that might have
been the first time Mom was ever on a movie set, but she was far

from intimidated. Mel Brooks and I were up by the camera. When he saw Linda, he said, "You have visitors."

We went back to where they were standing, and I introduced Brooks to my sainted mother. Without missing a beat, Mom said, "Your ass and my son's ass are the same distance off the ground." Rarely do you find Mel Brooks at a loss for words.

You know, it's a strange thing about *Blazing Saddles*: It is so brilliantly written that hardly a day goes by that I don't use at least one line from it. "Somebody go back and get a shit-load of dimes." "Are you out of your mind, can't you see this man is a ni—?" "Never mind that shit, here comes Mongo." "Hi, I'm parked over by the commissary." "Do do that voodoo that you do so well." "Shit, Bart, they said you was hung...." "And they was right." "This friggin' thing is warped." "Oh, what a nice guy." And the best musical line ever written, "They quote you Byron and Shelly and jump on your belly and bust your balloon." Well, you get the message. Rent the damn thing. Look at it and try to get through the next day without using at least one line. "More beans, Mr. Taggert?"

Boyhood Chums
Attack the President

---

*Life pursues me like a fury. Everything, at
all times, I am feeling, thinking, hoping,
hating, loving, cheering. It is impossible to
escape.*

—*W.N.P. Barbellion*

THERE'S AN APPLE TREE up there in the woods. I'm not
going to tell you where. Only me 'n' Spider Allison know where it
is, and we're just not saying. I will tell you that it is near the new
high school.

Me 'n' Spider sat up in that tree and solved the problems of
the 1943 world. You could say that me 'n' Spider won World War II
in that tree. I flew a P38, but I believe Spider preferred the P40.
We sat up there and ate green apples, checking each bite for
worms, and filled our pockets. Me 'n' Spider never let the apples
ripen.

Sometimes I sat alone in that tree, and I looked out over the
neighborhood and thought about things. Sometimes I was a hero
and won the heart of Linda Migliore, the prettiest girl in the
fourth grade. Me 'n' Spider had our favorite branches. You could
sit there and lean back and not hang on. Boy, I loved that tree.

A couple summers ago I had just finished a picture and
stopped in East Liverpool on my way home. I had thought about
that tree often over the years, and decided to see if I could at least

Me 'n' Spider won World War II.

find the spot where it had been. Surely by now it was dead and gone.

Picking my way through the brush, I navigated on a nine-year-old's memory and there, by God, was our apple tree. It had borne fruit then fallen over, slowly and quietly, no doubt, because it was intact and just tilting down the hill. Out of the stump was growing a new tree—green and straight.

I sat up in that tilted old tree and ate green apples and checked each bite for worms, and thought about me 'n' Spider. I couldn't get my old P38 to fly like I used to, and I forgot what Linda Migliore looked like. And I missed Spider. But the apples tasted the same, and it was peaceful visiting a dear old friend.

I was doing a very bad, never-to-see-the-light-of-day pilot for Universal. We were shooting in Washington, D.C. The great thing was that I had a suite at the Watergate almost as big as my house. The bad thing was that I didn't have anyone to show it to—much less share it with.

We were doing some shooting at Bolling Air Force Base outside Washington, and the base civil engineer was Colonel Thayer "Spider" Allison, my best friend since 1937. Spider and I grew up and went through school together, and when we graduated, Spider went to Virginia Military Institute, and I joined the Navy.

We were shooting on a remote section of the base near the Potomac River, and working what is known as a split day; that is, we started to shoot at noon for some "day" sequences, we broke for "lunch" at six o'clock, then we shot "night" sequences until midnight. We needed some extra equipment for lighting, so Spider arranged for the Air Force to provide us with a couple of "cherry pickers," motorized units that would lift lights and a technician high in the air to light a large area.

About four o'clock Spider came by to see how we were doing, and finding everything AOK, he and I headed off to the officers' club for a libation. Or two. Roger that.

At six the company broke for lunch, leaving the area with all the equipment, both Universal's and the Air Force's, unattended. Spider and I decided to check on things, so we went out to the location only to find it surrounded by an armed and angry company of Marines.

It seems that next to the Air Force base was a Navy base, Anacosta Naval Air Station, with no fence between the two, and we were on Navy property. Also on that Navy property were the hangars that held all of the president's helicopters. Yes, the president's. The Marines saw no humor in the situation, but had no one in their group who outranked Spider. So they arrested us. They saluted the hell out of Spider, but they still arrested us. For reasons I have never been able to understand, Marines guard Navy bases. As we used to say when I was in the Navy: the Marines guard our gates, and have never lost one. We were unceremoniously stuffed into the back of a vehicle and taken to the duty officer at Anacosta. The duty officer was a young lieutenant who, because of the hour, couldn't find anyone on the base who outranked Spider.

Spider finally lost it. He screamed in the lieutenant's face, "Get Charley on the phone right now, you little asshole, or I'm gonna stuff your silver bar so far up your ass you'll use it as a night light."

"Yes, sir," the lieutenant sputtered. "Who's Charley?"

"Your commanding officer, you little fart. Do you have his home phone number, or do you want me to give it to you? Dial the number and give me the goddamned phone." When Spider got his buddy Charley on the phone, the two of them screamed and laughed at the absurdity of it all and two very pissed-off Marines drove us back to the shooting location. The company was not yet back from lunch, and to this day, Universal has no idea how close they came to an "incident."

My Romance

*Louis, I think this is the beginning of a
beautiful friendship.*
          —*Humphrey Bogart,* Casablanca

WHEN WE RETURNED to Hollywood to shoot interiors for
that ill-fated pilot at Universal, a fellow came over to me on the
stage and introduced himself. He was to become my next best
friend.

"My name is Richard Colla. I'm directing an NBC World
Premier movie of the week, and I'd like to talk to you about doing
it with me. I've heard about you, but I decided to talk to you anyway. Somehow I think you and I could play together." "Play together." Those were the two words that got my attention. Play
together.

Finally, I thought, someone who views this business as I do. I
think I'll give this guy a try.

We did the movie together, and have never gotten too far
apart since. That was over twenty years ago. The picture was called
The UFO Incident. It was great fun playing with Richard, and
about halfway through shooting he handed me a script, and said,
"This is our next project. We have very little money; it's for my
company. Please read it, and tell me you want to do it. It stars
Katharine Hepburn."

No mystery here. Just straight-ahead good sense, and Hepburn yet. I took the script home and found God. Here was a great and innocent script. Here was a script that had soul and truth and celebrated the best of humanity.

I told Richard I would do the picture for nothing. He said, "Good, because Hepburn feels the same way, and she's doing it for nothing." Off I went again into another labor of love.

The picture was called *Olly Olly Oxen Free*. It was the story of two young boys, one of whom had a grandfather who had been a barnstormer back in the old days. Grandpa is dead now, but his old hot-air balloon is out back in an old greenhouse and to honor him, the boys decide they are going to repair the balloon and fly it on his birthday. While looking for spare parts in a junkyard, they meet the owner, Katharine Hepburn. She is taken by what the boys want to do and volunteers to help them. Thus begins a wonderful adventure that celebrates the best of the human spirit.

We were preparing the picture at Culver City Studios, and I was putting the finishing touches on Miss Pudd's (Hepburn's) truck. It had to be a very special truck, and it took me a long time to find the right one. Richard had a 1932 Packard touring car in a garage up in Montana, so we shipped it to Hollywood. I had the back section removed and built in its place a truck bed with oak sides. Essentially we had a convertible truck with enough "character" to match that of Miss Pudd herself.

One morning Richard said, "Miss Hepburn is coming in today. Want to meet her?"

"Are you nuts? Who in this whole world wouldn't want to meet Miss Hepburn? But I would have worn nicer clothes if I knew she was coming in. Why didn't you tell me this yesterday? What do I call her? We are talking about Katharine Hepburn, aren't we? I only met one other legend before. That was James Cagney, and he…"

"Shut up," said Richard. "She's a nice lady, and you two will get along great. Just treat her as you would any legend."

She arrived right on time, driving the late Spencer Tracey's old Thunderbird. No fanfare, no fuss, just Katharine Hepburn unfolding herself out of an old car. I stood in the distance watching, too

*"Perfect," she said. "Does it run?" she
asked as she folded herself into the driver's seat.*

apprehensive to go up and introduce myself. I figured I should
wait for Richard to send for me.

He sent for me. Hepburn was as easy to meet and talk to as
your old Aunt Minnie. Great lady, great stock, great bones, great
face, and, dear heavens, that voice. "Would you like to see Miss
Pudd's truck?" I asked after I caught my breath. Out the door the
two of us went, and she laughed heartily when she saw the truck.

"Perfect," she said. "Does it run?" she asked as she folded herself into the driver's seat.

"Like a top."

"Let's see, is it first, second, third, and reverse like this? Let's
take it for a spin."

"Lead on," I grinned. And off the lot we go, tooling through
Culver City, Miss Hepburn at the wheel and I beside her grinning
foolishly. She was talking and shifting gears and waving at people
who recognized her. I, in the meantime, was having hell's own

time coming to grips with the fact that I was sitting in a 1932 Packard pick-up truck driven by Katharine Hepburn, who was actually talking to and relating to me. Look, Ma, I'm dancin'!

"I'm so tired," began the lady as she drove along. "Last night when I went to bed the neighbor's pool equipment began making an awful racket. They were away on vacation, so I had to climb over their fence and shut it off." Imagine a seventy-two-year-old lady climbing fences and working on pool equipment and talking about it as if she did this sort of thing every day. "I had just gotten settled back in bed when the timer on the stove went off. I never did like or even understand that goddamned stove, but I punched all the buttons until it went off. I finally got to sleep only to be reawakened by that damned timer buzzer again. No matter what I tried, it wouldn't shut off. So do you know what I did?" By this point I was so thunderstruck by all that was happening—horns honking, she waving and shouting greetings to all who saw her, and I holding on for dear life—I could only shake my head. "I got in the kitchen drawer and I got a hammer. Then I beat that goddamned stove to bits until the buzzer stopped!" No wonder the lady was tired. No wonder the lady is a legend.

Hepburn was probably the most independent person I ever met. If she came into a room when we were having a meeting, we would all jump up and offer her our seats. She always declined and folded that elegant frame onto the floor with her back against the wall.

She got Edith Head to do her wardrobe for *Olly Olly Oxen Free*, and we did some wardrobe tests to see how it looked on film. In the screening room were Colla, Miss Hepburn, Miss Head, and I. Head had gotten the high-necked blouses Miss Hepburn wore in *Rooster Cogburn* with John Wayne, plain black slacks, and an extremely tattered red sweater that had belonged to Spencer Tracey. She had also selected a large tan duster. It was perfect. However, she had chosen a large, floppy hat that I didn't think was right. So in the dark I spoke up and voiced my opinion. Silence. Finally, Miss Hepburn spoke up. "I think the young gentleman has a point." There I was telling the great Edith Head she done wrong. Another Kodak moment.

Olly Olly Oxen Free was a tough movie to shoot. There were two young boys, Miss Hepburn, a dog, and a hot-air balloon; no other cast members. A lot of the picture was shot in the balloon, and the dog was the only one smart enough not to fly in it. We made a dog suit and put it on my daughter, Stephanie, for the aerial shooting.

The climax of the film involved the balloon breaking through the greenhouse with the two boys and the dog on board, while Miss Pudd chased it through Napa Valley, driving her truck, finally climbing aboard near San Francisco Bay. They all sailed off over the Golden Gate Bridge, into the fog, down the coast and landed in the Hollywood Bowl during the finale of the 1812 Overture.

It was while filming in the Hollywood Bowl that I had a most unusual experience. In order to get the balloon to land on the stage, we had to cable it off to four power winches. One was over the shell of the bowl, two were affixed to large lighting towers on either side of the bowl, and the fourth ran up to the top of the bowl and up into the woods beyond.

We had the uninflated balloon lying over the uppermost seats. We had three thousand extras in the seats closest to the stage, and we had the Los Angeles Philharmonic Orchestra playing on stage. We also had a pyrotechnic outfit to set off fireworks for the big finale. This was all very expensive and nerve-wracking, but I'll never forget the feeling I had as I stood on the stage with Richard, listening to the orchestra, looking out at all those people, and realizing we had pulled it off for little money and with Katharine Hepburn. Richard was feeling the same surge of emotion, and we stood there grinning at each other like idiots. Even now, after all these years, one of us will bring it up in conversation, and we still get misty-eyed.

We began to inflate the balloon. It was beautiful as it rose into the summer evening sky. The orchestra was playing fanfares, the crowd was cheering, and the cable that went up to the back of the bowl got fouled in the trees.

"I'll get it," I said, proving once again that I belong in a home under professional care. Up to the top of the seating I ran, and I leaped into the woods, grabbing roots and bushes to aid my climb to the cable. The climb was up a pretty steep cliff, but I persisted, finally reaching the cable and clearing it from the offending tree. The balloon leaped majestically into the sky with two little boys, Stephanie in a dog suit and Miss Hepburn safely in the basket. Again the crowd roared, the orchestra played and I stood up on the cliff with tears in my eyes.

I fell off the cliff. Yes, without so much as a "by your leave" I fell off the goddamn cliff. I flipped over once and landed on my ass, but miraculously I was unhurt. Scared to death, but unhurt. And no one saw me do it. I was up there all alone living my own little drama, while everyone else was having a hell of a good time, but I was unhurt. I did, however, have a rush of adrenaline, and had to pee very badly. Since I was up there alone and in the dark, I peed.

When the balloon landed safely on the stage, hitting its mark to the proper cue in the music, Miss Hepburn crawled out of the basket beneath the rapidly deflating balloon. She pulled the two boys out and, after the cut, said to the audience, "This just proves that if you're crazy enough you can do anything." That about sums up my philosophy. We finished shooting at two o'clock in the morning and everyone went home happy.

The next morning I awoke with a very strange sensation. As I was coming out of my nightly coma, I became aware that my fingers were quite swollen. Understatement. My fingers were the size of Polish sausages. As I was blinking awake and pondering this apparition, I slowly became aware of yet another sensation in yet another part of my body. It was that part of my body that I had used the night before to relieve the adrenaline rush brought on by the fall.

I was now fully awake and trying to make sense of this. I waddled into the bathroom to inspect the damage in private. With sausage fingers, I exposed that other part. Forget sausage. I was looking at a Hebrew National salami. "Funny," I thought, "you don't look Jewish."

I had grabbed poison oak as I climbed that cliff, thus thrusting myself into Hollywood immortality. The news of my misfortune spread faster than my misfortune itself, and while I was taking steroid shots and still working, I was getting calls from girls all over town just wanting to look at it. Colla became my social secretary, but he made them promise not to touch it. My doctor, Nancy Parry, was in Europe at the time of my poisoning. But word got to her, and I received the following telegram:

"Peter Peter picked some poison. Peter then picked up his pecker. Poor, poor Peter. With warmest personal regards, your doctor."

Along toward the end of shooting, Miss Hepburn was being interviewed by someone who asked her what, exactly, did she like to be called. I loved her answer. She said, "Katharine is nice. My friends all call me Kate. But on this picture everyone calls me Miss Hepburn, and I rather like that."

On the final day of shooting we were at the Victorian house we had shot most of the picture in and around. We were shooting interiors, which was lucky because it was raining like crazy outside. Miss Hepburn, as she always did, backed the Thunderbird up the driveway. This time, however, she got the left rear wheel off the pavement into the planting. At the end of the day we were having a little wrap party on the front porch. The lady came over to me and whispered, "I hate goodbyes. I'm going to just get in my car and sneak away." When she started to drive off she discovered her car was stuck in the mud. Of course the noise of the spinning tires got everyone's attention. The grips went out in the rain right away to help, and as they were organizing the push, I walked over and opened the passenger door.

"It just goes to prove one thing..." I teased.

"And what would that be, young gentleman," she yelled through the downpour.

"Not even you can make a great exit every time." I closed the door and could see her through the rainy window pounding on the steering wheel and laughing.

After we wrapped, I got a handwritten letter from Miss Hepburn. If you came into my house, you would be hard pressed to know what business I'm in. I have never been comfortable with placing "trophies" around. There is, however, that letter framed and hanging. It speaks, I think, much more eloquently than I can about what it is an art director actually does. (Her reference to sweat has to do with our lighting the greenhouse through the glass, rendering it oven-like.)

9-6-1976
Dear Peter—

You have done a most ingenious and lovely and sensitive job. All your sets are so photogenic and imaginative. What a real contribution to the situation. Of course they made me sweat. But one doesn't remember her sweat, only beauty. Congratulations to you and many thanks,
Katharine

Denise Alexander, an actress best known for her long-running role on "General Hospital," was also a producer on the show. She and Richard Colla were just beginning a relationship other than professional at about that same time. Happy to say they are married now, but that I have been in love with her as well. Linda says she should be angry, but I show such good taste that she can't find it in her heart to chastise me, and Denise thinks I'm cute. The truth is, over the years the four of us have been close friends, and I'm sure we always will be.

Denise was responsible for putting together and producing another labor of love. It was a television movie for Lifetime called *Hidden in Silence.* We shot it a couple of years ago in the Czech Republic, about 100 kilometers outside of Prague, in the city of Hraditz Kralovey. Don't try to pronounce it; it took me two weeks to run it past my tongue.

Hidden in Silence was the true story of a teenage Christian girl (Kellie Martin) and her little sister who hid thirteen Jews in her attic for two and a half years, between 1942 and 1945, and saved them from the Nazi death camps. It was a very emotional time for all of us because some, who were still alive, including the Christian

Me, Denise Alexander, and Richard Colla in Hraditz Kralovey celebrating the end of Silence.

girl herself, were present during shooting. If scripts like that can't be labors of love, then we don't deserve to be in the movie business. I'm as proud of that piece as anything I have ever done. Thank you, Denise, for allowing Richard and me to go out and play.

Richard Colla and I have lost track of how many projects we have done over the years. We know it has been many, and we know we have had a great time doing each one. We also know that no matter how old and tired we get, when the recess bell rings, we're going out to play together.

Yankee Doodle Dandy on Sunday, Don King on Monday

---

*"I wish I hadn't cried so much!" said Alice,
as she swam about, trying to find her way
out. "I shall be punished for it now, I
suppose, by being drowned in my own tears!
That will be a queer thing, to be sure!
However, everything is queer today."*
—*Lewis Carroll*

LINDA AND I were standing out by the pool at David Doyle's house one sunny Sunday afternoon. David was having a house-warming party, and we were talking to him and David Huddleston. Doyle you will remember from the television series "Charlie's Angels," the gravely voiced connection between Charlie and the Angels. Linda had worked with him years earlier in summer stock in Ohio where she was singing me through college. I had recently done something with him, and we had renewed an old friendship. Huddleston and I had just finished *Blazing Saddles*, in which he played the mayor of Rockridge. We got to talking about what we were doing next, and I announced that I was leaving for Cleveland the next day to do a black gangster movie. I then launched into a very bad impression of James Cagney, complete with my teeth over my lower lip, hitching up my pants and saying, "You dirty rat."

When the thunderous applause finally died down, Huddleston asked, "Have you ever met Jimmy?"

"Yeah, right, Dave, Jimmy and I have lunch a couple times a week and talk over old times. He's retired and lives on a farm in New Jersey or some damn place, and I sure would love to meet him someday."

"He's in the living room. I brought him to the party. He's out here on the coast to receive an award from the American Film Institute. He's an old friend of mine. Wanna meet him?"

"Sure, Dave, if he's just there in the living room, it won't be too much trouble for me to stop by and swap a few yarns about the old days. Who do you think you're shitting, Huddleston? How come you never mentioned him before now? Man, you must really think I'm a dork to believe that crap."

"Come on, I'll introduce you guys. I should get him up off his ass anyway. He's too old to be sitting inside on a nice day like this. Hey, Jimmy, get your butt out here!"

Against my better judgment I was beginning to believe him. Could it really be true? Oh, shit, just go along with the gag. Everyone will get a laugh at my expense, and that will be the end of it. Then, out of the living room door walked James Cagney. That James Cagney. Still ramrod straight. Smiling at me. At me. David must have introduced us—everything was a blur—because I heard myself saying, "Son of a bitch, Mr. Cagney, sir, it's a huge fucking pleasure to meet you." As those less-than-profound words spewed forth from my ignorant and unworthy mouth, even I had a difficult time coming to grips with the splendor of my dialogue.

Jimmy—I was already on a first-name basis with him— pretended not to hear my brilliant outburst, stuck out his Yankee Doodle mitt and said "Pleasure to meet you, pal." Sheesh, he called me pal! Looking back on that afternoon, it amazes me that I can remember what happened, but after all these years and all these crazy experiences, it still sits there as clear and indelible as a sunset.

Monday evening I was on the red eye to Cleveland with Dick O'Connor the associate producer, Hal Galli, the production manager, and a strange dude named Don Williams, the writer and producer. We were off to make an epic called *Blood, Black and White.* I should have known better, but like some wag once said, "Truth is stranger than fiction." What I was about to go through was so strange that all I can say is, "you can't make this shit up."

Back in the early seventies the first-class sections of some airlines had stand-up bars with flight attendants acting as bartenders. I got behind the bar and began to serve as bartender to the first-class section and the flight attendant. It was a riotous flight, and when we got off the plane in Cleveland, we were carrying the flight attendant.

With this sort of start, I began another strange odyssey. In many ways it was the strangest of my entire career. The executive producer of the picture was a guy from Cleveland I had never heard of, and the film was being financed by a group of doctors from the Cleveland area. We checked into the downtown Sheraton, and the desk clerk said there was someone waiting for us in the coffee shop.

At a large red booth with a red telephone on the table sat a strange-looking black man. He was our executive producer. He had established this booth as our "office." I had never heard of this guy, but I was immediatly fascinated by his outrageous hair. He had a spellbinding way of speaking. Through the course of the day, I discovered that (1) he had done some hard time for beating a guy to death with his bare hands outside a bar, (2) he ran the "numbers" game in northern Ohio and Pennsylvania, and (3) he was in the process of establishing himself in the "fight game." He definitely qualified as the "Most Unforgettable Character" in *Readers Digest.* Who else, but Don King?

While I was trying to deal with these revelations, the *Cleveland Plain Dealer* was trying to deal with what Don King and Hollywood had in common. Within twenty-four hours of our arrival, the newspaper had published a long, prominent article asking why we were in bed together. It contained photographs of King and his "Mystery Farm" outside of town. King's wife, by the way, was a charming lady I shared coffee with in the kitchen of the "Mystery Farm."

I suspect that because of the negative press the *Plain Dealer* was laying on us, King was very interested in getting us and the group of doctors together so that the doctors could see that we were, indeed, legitimate Hollywood types. (Now there is an oxymoron if I ever saw one!) To that end, the day after our arrival he had set up a meeting for us with the doctor who had organized the financing.

Up a very long driveway we went in the middle of the afternoon to the stately home of one Dr. Rhodes. There we were: Don King, some very strange thug-like guy named Rich Giccetta, and the Hollywood dudes on display. I was the first one to the door, and as it opened I stuck the same hand out that just a few days before had shaken the hand of Jimmy Cagney, and said, "Hi, I'm Peter Wool—." That's as far as I got, as the gentleman, Dr. Rhodes, grabbed my hand and pulled me inside.

"Pete, you son of a gun, I didn't know you were going to do this picture. How wonderful. This is really good news! Come in, all of you, and welcome."

Doctor Richard Rhodes and I had grown up together in the same poor neighborhood in East Liverpool. His family, I think, was even poorer than mine. He and his brother, Frank, had beaten the odds and made something of themselves. In fact, Frank had gone to Kent State at the same time I did, and we met and had coffee quite often in the student union. He was a speech therapist, and he had advised me on how to handle a stuttering problem my daughter had after her little brother was born.

I was reeling from the completely unbelievable scenario that was playing itself out before my eyes. All of a sudden I was the apple of Don King's eye because the doctors were getting spooked by the negative press we were receiving and the head doctor and I were buddy-buddy. Suddenly it was I who gave this "something less than elegant project" some legitimacy.

How the hell could this be happening?

Did I mention that the driver who had driven us out there that day was an elegant gentleman who was taking time and limousine off from his duties as chauffeur for the mayor of Cleveland?

His name was Diz Long, and he was the driver for Mayor Stokes, the first black mayor of any major city in the United States. For the remainder of my time on the picture, which was short, indeed, Diz Long was my driver, and we went about in the mayor's limo. I have no idea how the hell the mayor was getting around.

During the next week and a half we careened around Cleveland looking at locations and generally behaving like this was the most normal picture in the world. That was during the day. At night the whole thing got curiouser and curiouser. Don King and Don Williams had us out every night to a different black club. In the roughest sections of town. In the roughest joints in town. With the roughest people in town. Truth is, it was kind of fun for a while to be the only white faces for miles in any direction. (I experienced this in Africa, years later, under entirely different circumstances.) My liver, on the other hand, was asking for equal time.

So there we were, this strange band of citizens living this day-and-night life. The press was breathing down our necks. The mayor's driver was driving me all over town. We were meeting prizefighters for lunch every day. We were preparing a very bad script using these poor unsuspecting doctors' money. Don King's wife was trying to get a hole dug on the farm so she could bury her prize bull, which had unexpectedly bitten the dust. The bourbon stock had gone up four-and-a-quarter points. Dick O'Connor and I were asking, "Is this show business, or what?"

Then Dick Rhodes called me and asked the question I knew he was going to ask: "Are you guys for real? Should we continue?" In good conscience, I could not let a friend invest his money in a project that, if it ever got made, I would not pay to see. Dick said he would sit on it a few more days.

Don Williams called me later that day and asked me to meet him at the Theatrical Grill on Short Vincent Street later in the evening. "I'm doing a radio interview on a local talk show. The show's over at nine. See you then."

"Hold it, sidewinder, I'm giving my liver the night off. You go and have fun. I gotta get some sleep."

The following morning I came down to the coffeeshop for breakfast. I stopped and picked up the *Cleveland Plain Dealer* on the way in and settled down, all alone, at our big red booth with the little red telephone.

Front page: "Movie Producer Jailed by Ex-wife for Back Child-Support Payments." Seems she heard him on the radio and sent the marshal over to the station with the papers, and Don Williams was cooling his heels in the slammer. It was plain to me that no medical dollars were ever going to be squandered on the epic *Blood, Black and White*.

Taking stock, I realized I was never going to be paid for this crime, and neither were any of my "legitimate Hollywood-type friends." We all had round-trip tickets home, however, so all was not lost. Could have been worse, I suppose.

I have worked with Hal Galli and Dick O'Connor a number of times since then. I have not laid eyes on Don Williams since. I see Dick Rhodes at all the class reunions. Rich Giccetta became Mohammed Ali's trainer for a while, then faded from view. And we all know what happened to Don King. I never did find out if his wife got the hole dug to bury the prize bull.

Africa

IT'S NIGHT. A dark, hot, dusty and lonely night. Out on the edge of Lagos, Nigeria, you might as well be out on the edge of nowhere.

You've been drinking cognac in a dive called the Bamboo Cabin, and its time to get out of there. The natives are getting as restless as you are. You're waiting. It seems you're always waiting. But the cognac has started to kick in, and it's good to be alone. The shortcut back to the flat is dark, no moon, no ambient light. The trail through the bush is dusty, and the shapes of the trees are close and menacing. Ahead, a fire in a steel drum is blazing, and two figures moving around it cause shadows to dig into shadows.

The smoke brings with it the smell of meat being hopelessly burned. You stop at the fire even though the heat adds to the oppressiveness. The men by the fire seem friendly, chattering away in Yoruba and laughing. If they notice your whiteness, they don't show it. A brief negotiation, and for one nira, dinner is served. Burnt meat, onion, tomato and bread wrapped in a newspaper you can't read, and you burrow back into the darkness.

Back at the flat you peel off the wet shirt and kick off the hiking boots, causing a small dust cloud. The flat: one room, linoleum floor, four bare and dirty mattresses in a row. One window with a screen over it.

The screen is not there to keep out flies and mosquitoes, that's impossible. Instead, it keeps out foot-long lizards. Fifteen or twenty are hanging there, eyeing the rolled up newspaper, or is it you?

One candle on the floor, standing on the remains of other candles and other nights makes the room bounce in its flicker. A warm bottle of Star beer, Nigeria's finest, sits among a half-dozen empties. In your camera bag is an opener, and you find it by feel.

You open the beer, spread out the newspaper you can't read on the floor, check out the lizards one more time, sit on the edge of the mattress, and begin to chew the meat.

For a fleeting moment there is the lonely realization that no one in the world knows where you are. You push the thought away and you eat.

FADE TO BLACK

I wrote that about twenty years ago, longhand on my old stationery. I wrote it as soon as I finished eating that meal by the light of the candle. I must have been feeling Hemingwayesque that night. I was over there on an ill-fated location scout for a picture that never got made. I was the only white guy for miles in any direction, and was never made to feel threatened or at risk. Lagos, Nigeria, was and still is, the most corrupt city in the world. Because of the poverty, crime was rampant, but I always felt protected by my African hosts. Now that I look back on it, I wonder why I felt that way.

The military was running the country, and in order for me to travel "officially" I had to pass muster with a number of "big-wigs." The minister of finance, the minister of internal affairs, and the minister of labor all held me at bay as I waited for an audience for two long weeks. They were also all generals, and with that title came a certain amount of arrogance. So I had to bite my tongue and wait. Finally, after being cleared through Interpol, I passed inspection. They gave me a Volkswagen bus, a driver, and a bodyguard named Hussain who was a lance corporal in the Nigerian Army and the heavyweight wrestling champion of Ghana. He spoke the most elegant English I had ever heard, and he had tribal marks carved into his forehead and cheeks.

My hosts were two Nigerians, Gregory Awasika, writer, director, producer, and Willy Omani, who claimed to be a prince of
something or somewhere—acting, and I do mean acting—as another producer. Omani was wonderful, but he had a flair for the
dramatic, a larger flair than I, an old Hollywood maven, was used
to seeing. Awasika was and is a wonderful person with a dream he
could not pull off. He lived in the United States, and was in fact
becoming a citizen. He had started his life in the U.S. working in
a 7-Eleven, and eventually became a bus driver for the MTA in
Los Angeles. He wrote his script in his spare time, as everyone
seems to do in Hollywood, and got some of his countrymen interested in financing it, whether they had the money or not. I still see
Awasika after all these years. Omani was killed under mysterious
circumstances, as many people in Lagos are.

Nigeria is about the size of Texas, and the mangrove swamps
of the south give way slowly to the Sahara in the north. We had
woven our way from Lagos, in the south, to the country's northern
border, to the city of Katsina, and into one of those nights that,
while you are living it, feels like a weird dream or a Fellini movie.

We arrived in town after dark, Awasika, Omani, the driver
named "Shadow"—yes "Shadow"—Hussain, and the white guy.
We had no place to stay and no hope of finding proper accommodations. We couldn't find a restaurant that was not lethal looking.
A restaurant in that part of the world is a space that someone has
set aside where they will serve you something you can put in your
mouth to sustain yourself. Just don't, for God's sake, ask what it is.
We over-washed, over-refrigerated Americans can die quickly
from this sort of diet. A quiet conversation with a local, and I
found myself being escorted into a candy store!

"What is this, Goobers and Raisinets for dinner, you guys?"

We walked right through the candy store to the back wall,
which had about a three-foot-diameter hole blown through it, and
the guys start climbing through.

"Wait for the peckerwood," and I climbed into a hole stranger
than any Alice ever dreamed of. On the other side was a nightclub
of sorts. There was a very bad rock-and-roll band playing down at

the other end of the one large room. The floor was dirt. Black, unhealthy-looking dirt. There were tables and chairs, but not one piece of furniture had a match. The roof was gone. I don't mean just gone, it had fallen in sometime in the distant past. There were still dangerous-looking shards of roof just hanging there. God's beautiful sky showed through the outlines of the splintered ceiling. Most everyone in the joint was passed out on something and either lying on that awful dirt floor or sitting at a table with his head resting in his arms. Hussain threw two gentlemen thus engaged out of their chairs, thereby providing us a proper place to sit. That was the first time in my life I was terrified, truly terrified. We sat in this place and drank warm brandy for about an hour. Then, in my sweetest voice, I announced that although I had had nothing to eat and did not know where I was going to sleep, I was most afraid of being murdered in the shadows of this hole, and if we didn't get the fuck out of there right then, I was going to start taking slaves.

We drove to an abandoned military base. It was our only hope of finding a place to sleep other than the Volkswagen. There were rows of old barracks, inside of which were rows of beds and mattresses—dirty mattresses with mosquito nets over them. There was no electricity, but someone found some candles. As everyone was getting undressed, I decided to explore the rest of this building just to see what it was like to be a Nigerian soldier. I went down a long hall and into a small room. In the room was a large bathtub, and at the end of the tub there was a hose bib sticking out of the wall. I hadn't had a bath in three days, and I promised God that if He would just allow water to come out of that hose bib, I wouldn't take slaves.

Water, clean, clear water, sprang forth. I took off my clothes, wadded up one of my socks, and stuffed it into the tub drain. I emptied the wax from the cup in the candle and pressed the base of the candle into the soft goo. I climbed into the tub, and lay back like the prince Willy claimed to be, closed my eyes, and blew out all the air I had been storing up all night. And I grinned. In the grinning silence that surrounded me I could hear a clicking sound all around the tub. It became so loud and insistent that I was forced to pick up my candle and locate the source. Before me were hundreds of roaches. They were coming out of the hole in the tub where, under more civilized conditions, the real faucet would have been. What I did next shocks me to think of today, but it is amazing what the human brain can accomplish, and how adaptable we can become. I used the flame on my candle to herd the cockroaches back into the hole, and I took the chewing gum from my mouth, spread it out and plastered it over the hole. I then settled back and spent the next half-hour in as much bliss as I could muster.

I went to bed with a clean body on a dirty mattress. I pulled the mosquito netting over me, and in so doing trapped a very angry mosquito that spent the night dining on me. The next morning, in the light of day, there he hung on the inside of the net, bursting with my blood.

Hussain carried a gun. It was a very large silver pistol. The barrel was at least a foot long. "Hussain, old pal, give me that widow-maker for just one short minute." I shot that son of a bitch mosquito and blew my blood all over the net and blew a twelve-inch hole in the barracks.

Two years later I was dying from the flu. That mosquito had the last laugh. It gave me a rare bush typhus that took away my immune system. My doctor, Nancy Parry, checked all my fluids and found nothing wrong. As I began to get sicker, and considerably weaker, Nancy, who was also a drinking buddy, and who would still be my doctor if she hadn't moved back to Idaho, started to check disease symptoms common to places my travels had taken me. Thank God she was persistent. She found it, isolated it, and found a blessed antibiotic that beat it back. She found it after she had tossed my little pink butt into the hospital. It took years to recover fully. For the record, the official name of the disease is *Orientia tsutsugamushi.*

When we left the army barracks after the shooting, we returned to a city we had passed through a few days before. I had remembered it and thought it might be a good place in which to shoot most of our picture. The city of Daura contained some 100,000 souls, I was told. All the buildings in the city were made of mud, quite elegantly constructed, I might add, and thus were the same color as the ground on which they stood. No building had more than one story, so from a high vantage point the city was quite a sight. We arrived back there on a Friday afternoon, and there was some sort of festival going on. All 100,000 people, it appeared, were in the large square in the center of town. On a makeshift stage stood the local emir and, I found out later, a visiting emir. Their speechmaking had just ended, and they were getting into their respective Mercedeses to go back to the emir's palace (also made of mud, and painted in primary colors). We drove the VW into the middle of the crowd, and I got out to mingle with the locals. There were jugglers, dancers, guys with indigo dust splattered on their faces, and the local police, wearing green and red robes.

As the Mercedeses made their way through the crowd, the police opened a path. When the throng parted and the cars came past, there were probably forty people between me and them. I was told later that when the local emir got out of his car at the palace, he turned to one of the guards and asked, "Who's the white guy?" The guards found us as we were photographing the town and asked me, in good English and very politely, if I would mind meeting with his honor.

I was ushered into the palace and into a most unusual room, and came face to face with the big guy. It turned out that he had been educated in England and was a very personable guy, indeed. The room had beautiful Oriental rugs over the mud floor and lots of pillows piled about, on which we lounged while sipping Courvoisier. I felt like a pasha.

When he found out I was from Hollywood, the emir became really interested in me. I told him that, as much as I would like to shoot in his lovely city, it would be impossible because there were no hotel accommodations. I would need to provide rooms with proper bath facilities for at least forty people. I would also need tested water and offices and a dining facility, as well as security.

In the following two hours we made a deal. It turned out that he needed that same kind of space in which to install visitors. If the movie went ahead, I would design a hotel and have it built on property I chose within the city. The emir would pay for the hotel construction, less what it would have cost us to pay for hotel rooms while we were shooting there.

I went back to Lagos, designed a hotel with the rooms and facilities we required, and put it out to bid with three local contractors. At the top of all three bids was a figure representing my payment from them if I gave them the contract. In other words, my "payoff." Africa.

I'm sorry for Awasika that the picture never got made, but the trip was undoubtedly the best thing that ever happened to me. If you ever hear the words, "Who's the white guy?" you know they're talking about me.

The Day After

*A loud voice cannot compete with a clear
voice, even if it's a whisper.*
                    —*Barry Neal Kaufman*

OVER THE YEARS, I've done a great number of movies of the week for Bob Papazian, so when he calls it's not a surprise. It's always a pleasant time working with Bob, always a lot of laughs. He started his career as a page at CBS, came up through the ranks, and has certainly paid his dues. We have maintained a pretty good friendship over the years. So whenever we begin a new project we both know that we can have some pretty uproarious lunches and dinners for the next few months, as well as share a healthy hatred for whatever director he was dumb enough to hire.

He handed me a script and told me the director was Nicholas Meyer. Meyer had written the book *The Seven Percent Solution* and although he had directed only one film, a comedy, he was known around town as an intellectual. Thank you, Bob, for another untested director, who thought himself divine. That turned out to be the least of my worries. The television film was *The Day After* and, because of its message on nuclear war, it was in the news from the time we started to shoot until its broadcast on that fateful Sunday night. We were all agreed that we would tell the truth about what happens in a nuclear war. It is an awful and ugly truth. No one wins, and it ain't pretty. But we were dedicated to a good and truthful script, so off we trooped to Lawrence, Kansas, where the script was set, to spend a fun-filled summer recreating the end of the world.

It was the worst summer of my life. I had no idea how emotional it can be to spend a whole summer creating death and destruction. Just going through all the research before you put one of your own images on the screen is a daunting prospect. All the facts are so matter-of-factly printed that I began to lose my perspective. I began to believe we were actually going to war. I talked about it to everyone and anyone, ad nauseam. I had become fairly obsessed by the time shooting began. Papazian had thought about this and did the nicest thing. It seemed there was a group of doctors and psychiatrists who studied tragedies and natural disasters and their effect on the human psyche. He had a few of those guys around for us to "talk to" when we needed it.

Truly, we were not doing your average picture. We all hoped that maybe, just maybe, we could get people to talk to each other. We figured that if all the Big Dudes were looking eye to eye and talking, they wouldn't want to send us all to hell so easily. I like to think that in some small way we helped accomplish that.

Late one sunny Kansas morning I was standing in a field of wildflowers in an area down by the river that runs through Lawrence. A great arched bridge was in the top of my frame, and I was sketching a set I was planning to put there. It was listed in the script as a tent city, but my sketch was turning into much more. Before my eyes a field of wildflowers was becoming a smoke-and-debris-choked gathering place for a number of victims who were unlucky enough not to have been blown to bits in the blasts. Dying people with haunted eyes were burying the dead with vacant eyes in a common grave. A mother sat under a tin lean-to holding her dead baby. In that field of wildflowers there was no green, the dirt was black, and every natural or man-made thing on the dirt was black. I finished the sketch and walked off the field. I was afraid to turn around for fear the wildflowers would be gone.

I went back to the hotel intending to do a "neater" sketch.

When I opened the sketch book, the sketch was more terrifying than I remembered. I decided to let the crew work from it. It might inspire them. Mort Zwicker, my construction coordinator, came slamming into my room. "Well, boss, what are we doing to-day?" I pointed to the sketch leaning on the television. Mort's face got ashen, and he went into my bathroom and threw up. So much for the glamour of filmmaking.

One more little story: That set got built just as my sketch showed. The day we began shooting the scene, I walked up onto the bridge to get a bird's-eye view. There was an ancient Asian lady standing there quietly. As I walked up to the rail next to her I noticed that she was crying. She felt my gaze and looked over to me. All she said was, "I was there." It was a strange compliment, but I will always think of it that way.

Annie, Dom, and Me

> *That is the way with poetry: When it is incomprehensible it seems profound, and when you understand it, it is only ridiculous.*
>
> —*Galway Kinnell*

WHEN ANNE BANCROFT wrote *Fatso* and was planning to direct it for 20th Century Fox, she asked me to design it. *Fatso* was a charming little piece she had written for Dom DeLuise: a love story, sweet and gentle, about the Italian love for food weighed against the love of a lady. It was the perfect vehicle to showcase DeLuise's considerable talent as a serious actor, not just a comic.

It was obvious to me from the start that I had to treat this with loving care. I had to make all the actors, all New York Italians, by the way, including Bancroft, who was also acting, feel at home in their surroundings. I went back to New York and visited the house where DeLuise had grown up. His mother still lived there. Since cooking was such an important part of the story, I paid special attention to the kitchen. I did not want to "reproduce" the apartment; we had shooting considerations, and actor and camera positions to think about. I did, however, want the kitchen to be as close to DeLuise's own kitchen in "feel" as I could get it.

Normally kitchens and bathrooms are not "practical" in movie sets. Unless the action calls for it, there is no need to call in a plumber to make all the sinks and toilets actually work. Refrigerators are almost never cold, and stoves and ovens are rarely called upon to perform on camera. Cooking is almost always done off camera and set into place for the filming. Movie magic. The kitchen I designed for DeLuise, however, was "practical." Everything worked. The 'fridge was cold, the gas stove worked, and the sink had hot and cold running water.

Kitchen cabinets are also usually fake. If the action calls for one drawer to be opened, chances are that drawer is the only one that actually works. The rest of them are simply "plant-ons." All my kitchen cabinets worked.

We also built an industrial-type kitchen on the stage so that we could have food cooking at all times. Just to walk onto the stage started hunger pangs because of the smell of tomato sauce simmering in a pot in one of the two kitchens. Annie invited anyone who wished to create any of his favorite Italian recipes anytime he cared to. We were all eating all the time. Hardly anyone actually went to lunch. I gained ten pounds; it was heaven.

When we finished construction I asked the set dressing and property departments to bring in everything for the kitchen and leave it all in boxes in the middle of the room. In came pots, pans, dishes, glassware, silverware, the plastic silverware holder, serving ware, dishtowels, and bags of groceries.

The cast was in rehearsal, so I went by and told DeLuise I needed him on the set for at least an hour after rehearsal.

"What the hell for? I'm tired. Why do you need me today?"

"I need you today so the milk won't go sour and the fruit spoil," I answered. "Besides, you'll thank me for what I'm gonna have you do." Annie knew I was going to do this, and she just smiled at him.

I heard Dom coming through the stage door. "Okay, Wooley, let's get this, whatever it is, over with." As he walked onto the set for the first time, he stopped short. He looked around at his apartment and his eyes got wet. "Hey," he said, "this is my place!"

"You're gonna be spending many days in this kitchen. It's

important to me that you are as comfortable as possible. I want you to put all this stuff away. We'll have fun."

Dom began to blubber and sniffle. He kissed me and went to work. He put everything where he wanted it. I hung the towel rack were he thought it should be. He really got into it, and when he closed the refrigerator with his foot, I, and he, knew he was home. All the time he was putting things away, I was sitting at the kitchen counter and we were talking like two old friends. We were talking about everything but what he was doing. He was putting his kitchen together without any help from me. Never once did he ask where I thought something should go. He was home.

The kitchen window over the sink looked out over some fake greens and a painted backing. The last thing he did, which almost made me cry, was pick up a not-quite-ripe tomato and place it on the window sill.

Lanced in the Heart

Beware what you set your heart upon.
For it surely shall be yours.
                                        —Ralph Waldo Emerson

Part One

MY AGENT CALLED. "Do you know a Lance Hool?" Sounded a lot like a medical term to me, but, no, I didn't know a Lance Hool. An HBO script arrived, a western, called, *The Tracker.* Damn, I had been wanting to do a western for a long time and here was a wonderful script that reminded me of the old John Wayne classic *The Searchers.*

Soon I was in a meeting with Lance Hool and the director, John Guillerman. Guillerman was a curmudgeon from England who had just directed the remake of *King Kong* for Dino Delaurentis, and before that, *The Towering Inferno* for Irwin Allen. He seemed a pleasant enough person, and Hool was a beauty. I told them that if they wanted me, I would need the weekend of May 23 off. My son, Christopher, was getting married. My wife and I were hosting a rehearsal dinner on Friday night, and the wedding was on Saturday evening. "I only have one son, and he is important to me. No movie is going to keep me away from such an event. So if you want me, you are going to have to do without me on that weekend."

"No problem," they both agreed. "We have to keep our priorities straight. A movie is only a movie."

I started scouting all over the Southwest and eventually narrowed it down to northern New Mexico and southern Colorado.

On the Friday of the fateful weekend, I found myself sitting down to breakfast with Guillerman in a hotel coffee shop in Taos, New Mexico. "Look, dear boy," John said, "it would be much better for all of us if you skip the rehearsal dinner, scout all day today and tomorrow, and we'll get you home in time for the wedding." My eggs were cold when they arrived at the table, so I knew I wasn't missing much, and this would be a good time for one of those "Peter Wooley Major Events." Slamming down my napkin on top of my cold eggs, I said, "Fuck you, John, I'm outa here." I got in the rental car, drove back to Albuquerque, called Hool in Los Angeles, told him what had happened, and suggested he might want to find another production designer. He was very embarrassed and said that, no, I should come into the office Monday morning and he would see that it all got straightened out. When I arrived at LAX he had a limo waiting for me. Classy guy.

It was a great wedding. My son was properly wed and on Monday morning, into the office I went. The first person I saw was Guillerman, who, as always, was wearing his uniform: Levis and a white t-shirt. I have never seen the man in anything else. Always clean and neat, but never a variation. "Nice shirt," I said to him, heading for the coffeepot. "Thank you, dear boy," he said, and the incident was never spoken of again.

What we had that Friday morning was a pissing contest, and I won. I not only won the round, but I won his heart. John Guillerman was not used to having people challenge him. He challenged everyone he worked with, including the actors, and everyone always blinked first.

It got to the point where Kris Kristofferson, who was starring in the film, would come to me and say, "You gotta stay on the set more."

"I can't, Kris, I have too much work to do. Besides, why do you need me on the set?"

"He behaves himself when you're around. When you're gone, he gets impatient with all of us and gets himself in a snit."

"Snit, shit, Kris, you handle it. Your name is over the title. You're a big star, and David Huddleston is a big star and Scott Wilson is a big star. You're on your own." And all along Hool, the producer, was standing back laughing. He and Guillerman were good friends, and he didn't take any of this silliness to heart.

As time went on, however, it was I who kept Guillerman in line and in reasonable spirits. Until one morning. We were scheduled to shoot two scenes along the Rio Grande outside of Santa Fe. One scene was scheduled for the morning, and the other for the afternoon. When we arrived that morning, the owner of the property, not knowing what we had planned to do, had taken out all the small trees and brush in the exact spot we wanted to shoot. Of course, Guillerman went ballistic, screaming and waving his arms like a madman, and of course wanting to blame me; but he couldn't find the words.

"Listen, John, you go on down the river, it's just two hundred yards, do the afternoon's work, and in the meantime, I'll put trees and brush back here and make it look like this never happened."

"How will you do that, dear boy?" he whined.

"My problem, not yours, John. Now run along and leave this to me."

It was a monster of a job, but my construction coordinator, Chip Raedelli, and I ran all over a place to find brush and small trees we were allowed to cut down, and we got the set looking great.

After lunch, back came the company. They were oohing and awing, and the actors were on their horses ready to go. Guillerman, in the meantime, was standing behind a small tree with about a four-inch trunk we had placed there. He had a pained look on his face as he said to me in his most exasperated voice, "But right here is were I want to put the camera, dear boy."

I walked over, tore the tree out of the ground and threw it at him. I fully intended to hit him with it and hoped to hurt him. All

I really did was frighten the horses and cause the actors, who were laughing hysterically, to hold on for dear life.

That night in the hotel, Linda and I were walking out of the dining room when I heard that voice across the room. "Come over, dear boy, and have a drink with my wife and me."

As we sat down, Guillerman said to Linda, "Did he tell you what he did to me today?" Linda gulped and nodded. "Don't you love the passion?" he asked, with a dreamy look in his eyes.

Between you and me, by the time that picture was finished I would have killed to work with John Guillerman and Lance Hool anytime they wanted me.

There was a young Ute named Arthur Badback who helped us out from time to time. His dad was the tribal chief, and since we were shooting a good portion of the picture on Ute land, it was prudent to hire as many Utes as we could afford. I took a liking to Badback, but he wasn't what you would call a big talker.

One day we were shooting on two different locations on Ute land. The location manager, Tony Schweikle, made arrangements for us to move from one location to the other at about two o'clock in the afternoon. Arthur and I were sitting along a dirt road looking out over a truly beautiful view in the Four Corners area of Colorado. Two o'clock went to three o'clock then to four. After a full two hours of silence, Arthur turned to me and in that Native American cadence said, "Ever been to New York?"

"Oh, yes, my wife used to live there just before we were married. As a matter of fact, I have made a couple of movies there. Man, I like New York."

. . . .

Forty five minutes later, Arthur turned to me and said, "Yep, the Big Apple."

Now that we were on a conversational roll, I jumped right in and said, "You know, Arthur, when the company finally arrives they're going to find two skeletons sitting here."

. . . .

A half-hour later, Arthur, without moving an inch said, "One have hat."

I have never really been sure whether Arthur Badback's conversational wizardry was an Indian thing or a youth thing.

Part Two

A FEW YEARS LATER Lance Hool called me again. "How would you like to spend four months in Acapulco?" It sounded good to me. The project was a comedy starring Martin Short and Danny Glover called *Pure Luck*. The director was a lady from Australia named Nadia Tass. She was Rebecca of Sunny Brook Farm: sweetness and light. Two weeks before shooting started, she began to change. Now all directors change a little when shooting starts. That's the nature of the beast. But Tass changed. When I think about it now the hair on the back of my neck stands up. Her voice, face, and body changed. Rebecca became Eva Braun, and she stopped talking to me. Why, I'll never know. She also stopped talking to Lance Hool.

I went to Hool and said, "This is very difficult. I'm not so sure I can go on with this madness."

He laughed and said, "Do what I did; get an emissary to act as a go-between."

Boy, now I've heard everything. But, what the hell, Acapulco is Acapulco, after all, and I might not pass this way again. I assigned my Mexican art director, Hector Romero, to the task. He took on the job gleefully, and all went well, albeit stressfully.

Toward the end of shooting I decided it was time to reapproach the good Miss Tass, and see if her attitude had perhaps taken a turn for the better. We were shooting in a jungle hospital I had built in the forest outside of Acapulco. It was a wonderful set. It was neat looking and easy to shoot, and it was perfect for the picture. The last set we were shooting in Acapulco was another hospital I had built in the mission style on a river. It was now in the process of being painted and aged. So out to the jungle I went, with Romero in tow to present myself to the lady. With an olive branch in my mitt, I confronted the lady on the porch of the hospital. She looked at me, and that change began to spread around her. Her eyes darkened and her shoulders drew up in a knot. In a voice that rattled the landscape she roared, "I hope you enjoyed your vacation." I ignored the comment, and asked if she had any comments about the mission hospital. "I want it yellow!" she screamed.

"Yellow," I said, and walked away with my olive branch up my ass. Hool thought my gesture was noble, and he was truly apologetic about the way she treated me. But painting a Catholic mission hospital on a remote river yellow put a huge strain on my creativity.

It certainly did not affect my relationship with Hool, but I did chide him more than once on his taste in directors. I even suggested that since directors are required by film bonding companies to take physical exams before shooting begins, he might consider sticking a Rorschach Test under their noses at the same time.

Tass, it seemed, lacked one essential requirement of a comedy director. She had no sense of humor. Insanity is allowed, but lack of humor cannot be tolerated. Shooting sixteen takes is not good when directing a comedy. It is also essential to know when something is or isn't funny. Poor Nadia Tass should never have been hired by Universal. I'm sure that accounted for part of her madness.

While I was in Acapulco I painted a picture of her. I was trying to exorcise demons. I called it "The Lady Wants It Yellow." I got it home and couldn't stand to look at it, so I painted a portrait of myself over it. Sort of poetic justice. It is currently hanging in my office.

Wherever Nadia Tass is today (and I hope it's not near me, or even in this country) I pray she has turned back into Rebecca.

Part Three
FIVE YEARS WENT BY, the phone rang. It was Lance Hool. "Wanna do it again?" This time it was back to Mexico to do a historical film based on the Irish involvement in the Mexican-American war. It was a script right on the edge of brilliant, and I couldn't wait. However, wait I did. I waited eight months as they kept saying, "Any day now."

The first thing I asked Hool was, "Who's directing?"

"I am," he grinned. I allowed as how that was the best move he had made since our relationship began. What's that timeworn expression? "Little did I know."

Finally I got a call to go to Mexico and begin scouting. So off I went to Mexico with Hool, his brother, Conrad, who was producing, and my old pal from *Pure Luck*, Hector Romero to do *One Man's Hero*. Good script, nice people, and I was doing Fred Astaire singing, "Heaven, I'm in heaven...."

Once we had decided on locations, Romero and I settled down in Durango and began the design process. Ten weeks later I still had not been paid, my per diem payments were way behind, and I was running out of money from paying petty cash out of my own pocket. My wife was hysterical, my agent was incensed, and I was on the verge of "amok."

We were understaffed, did not have enough construction people, and we were turning out magnificent sets. We were building walled cities, dams, bridges, whole towns to be burned down, and battlegrounds.

The shooting company finally came down ready to begin principle photography, and with them came this stranger. He looked just like Lance Hool, and he sounded just like Lance Hool, and everyone called him Lance. He even said his name was Lance, but I don't now, nor did I then, believe that to be true. He turned into the male version of Nadia Tass, with one extra added attraction: he also became the most imperious soul I have ever run across. After thirty-three years of doing this, I was completely turned around. How could a person whom I had known all those years as a first-rate producer become a third-rate director right in front of my eyes?

As the pundit says, shit happens. And happen it did.

After going through over ten months of waiting, working, begging, and watching my blood pressure hit 180/120, I realized I was still capable of making bonehead career moves, and I ran like a thief. In my "goodbye memo" I said, "Ten months and not a minute more." My design work was finished, and Hector was more than capable of seeing that what few things remained got completed. They saved a fortune by not having to pay me for the last eight weeks of shooting, and now, in their eyes, they had some one to blame for everything that went wrong. That was an option I'm sure they picked up.

Actually, the way I see it, Lance just has really shitty taste in directors....

Did You See What He Just Put in His Mouth?

Some people never go crazy,
What truly horrible lives they must live.
—Charles Bukowski

MY SECOND PICTURE with Mel Brooks was *High Anxiety*. We had a running gun battle going since *Blazing Saddles* about Brooks not getting in touch with me to do a picture until the last minute, when I was busy doing another project. And "Dammit, Mel, if you give me a couple months' notice, I'll arrange to be available." This, incidentally, is an ongoing problem in Hollywood; it is almost impossible to arrange your life.

Linda and I were vacationing in the Florida Keys, and Brooks called. "I'm sending you a script. Read it. Try not to move your lips so much as you read it; it makes you look dumber than you are, if that's possible. I love you. Did I call on time?"

The script was a send-up of Alfred Hitchcock. It was full of scenes from Hitchcock's more memorable films wrapped around the plot of a prominent man being held in a mental institution against his will. The institution's name was The Psychoneurotic Institute for the Very <u>Very</u> Nervous. Even carved in the entrance sign, the second "Very" was underlined.

My first day on the Fox lot I went into Brooks's office and, after obscenities, insults, small talk, and pleasantries were exchanged, he slid a piece of paper across his desk with all of

Hitchcock's films listed on it. "Which of these do you want to look at?"

"All of them," I said. This was before everyone had VCRs, and I couldn't resist the opportunity to sit in one of 20th Century Fox's plush screening rooms for a week and watch Hitch do his magic. It was especially great sitting there alone and calling in on the intercom to the projectionist to tell him to run the previous scene back and play it ten more times. Imagine the workout I give my VCR these days. I really had fun doing that movie. I suppose that at that time in my career I was as close to movie Nirvana as one can get. For me it was the end of an era. After that, with very few exceptions, movie making seems more stressful, bottom-line oriented, and filled with young people going around selling ten-pound boxes of angst. If you couldn't afford to buy one, they gave it to you. It seems imperative now to consume at least two pounds of angst a day, or they won't think you're working. Working. There's that word again.

On *High Anxiety*, we worked, of course, but it didn't seem that way. I always felt more like I was playing. Brooks kept the writers on the set during production. "Comedy ain't funny," Brooks yelled quite often in mock hysteria. The written comedy line does not always translate to the spoken word, and it was comforting to him to have the writers around. It is especially comforting when you both are directing and acting. So all during production Brooks' writers—Rudy Deluca, Ron Clark, and Barry Levinson—sat in front of the video-assist monitor.

That was also back in the time when most of my work was completed by the time principal photography started, so I could spend most of every day beside the camera. I sat with the writers in front of the monitor. I was supposed to be looking for any visual problems, but that never stopped me from adding my two cents to the writers if they were discussing a script change. I must have done pretty well, because they tolerated me and we had a great time playing word games between takes.

Brooks would shoot three or four takes in a row, then come over to the monitor, replay them, and we would discuss which

Mel has the suit, but I have the hat.

takes to keep and which to throw away. As I said, for a hairy-legged production designer, this was about as close as I was ever going to get to Nirvana. Nowadays, it seems, I'm still running my ass off the last week of shooting.

Paul Lohman, the director of photography, had a motor home he kept parked outside the sound stage. Every morning he prepared bagels and great coffee, and he, Brooks, and I, and anyone else who was hungry, started our day in Lohman's tin house. We would laugh and talk about anything but the movie, then stroll onto the stage and begin the day's festivities.

In a scene from *The Birds*, the heroine is sitting on a park bench as birds begin to accumulate menacingly on a jungle gym behind her. They then attack her and force her to run. We were preparing a similar scene for our film with one not-so-minor variation.

The bird trainer simply had to train the birds to fly from their holding pen to a jungle gym. I built a special jungle gym with smaller crossbars to accommodate their little bird feet, then I put slots in the crossbars for bird seed to accommodate their little bird appetites. The birds couldn't wait to get to that jungle gym.

The variation on the scene was that the birds did not attack our hero, they flew over him, and—there's no dainty way to put this—they shit on him. The special effects man, Jack Monroe, was laboring in a little shop he set up in the corner of the stage working out how to manufacture and deliver such a special payload, and deliver it on an actor who just happened to be our boss.

Now who in his right mind would call this kind of thing a "job"? One day, Monroe came over to the monitor and whispered to me to step into his shop. He had set up a little show. He took a wax capsule and filled it with this suspicious stuff. He put it into a length of pipe and blew it out very fast onto the floor. Bird shit.

"What is that stuff, Jack?"

"Mayonnaise, some chopped spinach, and a pinch of tempura sauce," he said, sounding more like a chef than a special effects wizard.

"Okay, Jack, here's the deal. I'll go back and sit down..." Jack started to grin "...you quietly come in behind me so the guys can't see you, and when there is a lull in the conversation, you blow one of those at my feet."

It is very common for a bird of some type to make its way onto a soundstage, and we had a pigeon that enjoyed hooting in the middle of takes and driving the sound mixer nuts. He also left the real version of what we were manufacturing on the muslin ceilings. Usually the ceilings in sets are made of muslin. Everyone knew of the pigeon, and every one at one time or another had cursed it.

At the perfect time bird shit landed at my feet. The three writers jumped up. Have you ever noticed how, when a bird "surprise" lands someplace, everyone always looks up like they expect the benefactor to spin around and come in for a second pass? Now I was sitting there watching three writers standing up, looking up, and cursing. DeLuca, for some reason, was starting to edge toward the door. "Just a minute, you guys, let me check this thing out." I leaned over, scooped up the ersatz shit with my index finger, and with a lip smacking sound, ate it. "Yeah, that's bird shit all right." *Smack, smack.*

By now, DeLuca was racing toward the stage door, and Levenson was right behind him making gagging sounds. Clark was jumping up and down screaming, "I can't believe that even you would do something so loathsome just to get a laugh." They actually believed I would go that far for a laugh. They were almost right. Rudy Deluca used to say that the most "at risk" things at a party I was attending were the lampshades.

Action

I HAD CONCEIVED and directed a documentary and was spending my nights in a cutting room happily editing. My friend Bryan Hickox called me and asked me to direct a children's series for PBS in Austin, Texas. "We've been playing for years and I always wanted to give you something to direct. Children, puppets, animals—all the things they tell you never to try to direct, I want you to direct. God knows you have carried enough directors around. We'll fly to Austin for the next few weekends and cast this thing, and you'll have two more weeks to finish cutting your project."

What he didn't know was that I was also doing a movie of the week for CBS. During the day I was shooting *News at Eleven,* at night I would cut my documentary, *The Very Last Ride,* and on Friday evening I drove down to LAX, met Hickox, and flew to Austin to cast "The Real Adventures of Sherlock Holmes and Procter Watson." Friday night we usually had a meeting with the local PBS brass. Saturday and Sunday we would attempt to cast kids and fly back to LAX. I would jump in my car, and be in bed by midnight.

After three weeks of this, I was not far away from needing professional help. One Sunday night, as I was running through the

LAX parking garage with my car key in my hand, I found myself stabbing the key into that little piece of air where the car lock was supposed to be. "Some son of a bitch has stolen my car!" I screamed to all the other silent cars around me that hadn't been stolen. My new silver four-door Mercedes Benz was so beautiful and sexy I named her "Sinthia." "How could they do this to my Sinthia?" I moaned to the cars that hadn't been stolen, proving to them my need for a room in an institution. I then went to the police, who were not surprised that another Mercedes had been stolen from the airport. I took a taxi home and notified my insurance company, who arranged for me to fill out many forms and rent another car for the thirty-day waiting period you must suffer through.

In the next thirty days, I finished the documentary, the CBS movie of the week, and the ten-episode children's series for PBS. I returned home from Austin on the twenty-ninth day of my waiting period. A call came in that same day from the police at LAX. "Mr. Wooley, you'll be happy to know we found your car."

"Oh, great. What kind of shape is it in?"

"Dirty."

"Dirty?"

"Dirty. It hasn't been moved since you drove it in here on that Friday afternoon," the cop laughed. "You just forgot where you parked it. Oh, yes, and we are so happy about finding your car, we're waiving the monstrous parking bill you ran up. We would appreciate, however," he said roaring with laughter, "if you would please arrange to fly out of Burbank from now on!"

Directing turned out to be a scary and enlightening event. I felt like I was living in the center of a storm that I myself was creating. All creative decisions stopped at my door, and I kind of liked it that way. I did my homework and kept everyone informed, and I took the proper time with the actors. Actors ain't like us. They are special people with special skills and needs. If you think acting is easy, try it. That's why they are actors and we're not.

That doesn't mean they are as personally adorable as they would like you to think they are. Some of them, I truly believe, live on the outskirts of madness. It is the nature of the beast.

Get that kid out from under Sherlock's truck!
(With Leo Eaton.)

The good news was I was working with children who were not sophisticated. The bad news was I was working with children who were not sophisticated. My entire crew was videotape-trained, instead of film-trained. I wanted to shoot in film technique using tape because film technique was what I understood. It was like learning to fly at night, and I was in heaven.

There was an executive at the PBS station in San Antonio who had been an assistant director for the BBC in London. I'm sure they assigned him to me as my assistant director because of his experience and my lack thereof. Never mind, Leo Eaton became a very good friend and workmate. Many an evening Leo, Bryan, and I spent in the hotel bar drinking wine, eating pistachio nuts and planning the next day's work. We bonded.

One evening toward the end of the shoot, Leo began telling me of this project he was about to mount for the PBS station in Maryland, and being a history nut I was captured. "It's six half-hour shows in newscast format of six events that helped shape the world," Leo started. "We will shoot them in Spain, Turkey, and on the Isle of Man in the Irish Sea. We'll try to shoot as much of it as possible where it happened. The six newscasts will start with the Battle of Hastings in 1066, include the sweep across Europe of the Mongols, the crusades, Black Death, the fall of Byzantium, and end with the fall of Granada in 1492." He was directing it and wanted me to design it and act as sort of de facto producer.

"Just let me know where and when, pal, and I'm your man." Just before Christmas the following year, Leo called me.

"I'm flying out from Maryland to spend a couple of days with you working on the script. Plan to be in London after the first of the year. We'll include a full set of business-class air tickets for Linda in your contract." In case you have lost track of my ego, I'm here to remind you that it was working at full speed.

The following February, I headed off to London via the polar route to begin "Timeline" with Leo Eaton for PBS. It was a harrowing, humbling, and joyful experience. We were to shoot parts of six half-hour shows in three countries. We were going to shoot them all at once. That is, we were not going to do the first one, finish it, then go on to the second. Instead we were going to shoot bits and pieces of each one in all three countries, and we were doing them as a co-international production with Spanish Public Television, Turkish Public Television, a production company in London called Holmes Associates, Maryland Public Television, and Southwest Texas Public Broadcasting. In London we set about getting together a group of department heads who would make the whole trip with us. Our producer was an Australian living in London. Our writer/director was a Brit living in the United States (Eaton). The cameraman was a true Brit. The costume designer was a Visigoth Spaniard living in Madrid. The head of hair and makeup was a Greek Cypriot, and of course there was me.

We were to arrange our shooting schedule, travel to all three countries, and hire in each of these countries a production unit who would do the work. I had art directors in Spain, England, and Turkey. Each had construction and decorating crews, and I was flying from country to country making my needs known in three languages. In the six months it took to prepare and shoot the series I learned the true meaning of the word "patience." We actually pulled it off, and those videotapes are in many school curricula as teaching aids after having aired on the PBS network a number of times.

I had a charming Spanish art director. He was older than I and he smoked a pipe. As pipe smoking goes more and more out of fashion I have noticed that pipe smokers today are more and more often either dilettantes or self-important assholes. This charming fellow was both. He was a great painter, and he painted a picture of a street I had chosen as a location for the "Black Death" sequence. We were shooting in a small town called La Alberca up in the mountains near Portugal. The painting hangs in my den today, and I really love it. It reminds me, however, of what he could have done for the picture if he had put his head to it. I could never get him to do his work with the construction and set dressing people until the company was standing on the location ready to shoot. He said that was how they did it in Spain, and I allowed as how that was why Spain had such a lame film community. Every morning was like having a root canal. I finally beat everyone into submission and got them to start preparing the sets the day before. So we survived Spain, at least, and moved on to Turkey.

My Turkish art director was a pretty little thing from Istanbul who had a thing going with the Turkish production manager. I took my interpreter and crew to the island we were shooting on in the middle of the Aegean Sea. She stayed in Istanbul to supervise the construction of some rather large and complicated props we needed. I had sat in Istanbul and designed all the things I wanted her to build, then left for the island with the gang. My helpers in Turkey were called set-techs, and they were truly wonderful. There were twelve of them ranging in age from eighteen to sixty, and there was nothing they wouldn't attempt to do. No one spoke a word of English, so I had to communicate everything through an interpreter. Actually, it was quite easy because they were so willing to do anything. They built the sets, threw down their hammers, and painted. When that was finished, they decorated the sets, then

*What all respectable production designers
wear on location in Istanbul.*

got into wardrobe and worked as extras. They did everything with
such gusto, and they did everything like they were acrobats, complete with the whoops and hollers you hear when acrobats do their
thing. I called them the Fabulous Flying Zambini Brothers, and
they thought that was great. They would pound their chests and
yell, "Zambini."

I told them when we first started construction on the island
that I need some telephone poles. Their transportation consisted
of a farm tractor pulling a small trailer. When I mentioned the
poles, they started to whoop and yell, leaped onto the tractor and
trailer, and disappeared in a cloud of dust. They were gone about
an hour, and I heard them yelling and laughing before I saw them
return. They had about ten telephone poles stacked in the little
trailer. I looked at the bottom of the poles and they all had fresh
saw cuts on them. I never had the heart to ask them where the
poles came from.

When we wrapped the shooting in Turkey, I threw a party for them in Istanbul. I took over a pub and we had a slobbering good time. One of them said to me that day, with tears streaming down his face, that he and the rest of the Zambinis would go anywhere in the world to work for me again. I confess to tearing up, myself.

The art director, on the other hand, showed up on the island just before we started to shoot with none of her work completed. When I tried to fire her, I got my first taste of Asia Minor philosophy. The production manager said, and I quote, "I cannot fire her because I hired her, and it would be admitting I made a mistake." When the shock of that wore off, I asked him to please keep her away from the set and from me so that I wouldn't have to look at her. This he could do. I called London in the meantime and had my English art director fly in. She was a great lady who delivered everything she said she would, and called me an "old fossil." God, I loved that lady. She was just under six feet tall, wore proper English shoes, and could drink the English construction crew under the table.

I learned a great deal about the art of "sticking together." One of the many wonderful things about this business of show is how well those of us who have done it for a long time know how to use each other and when to jump in and help. Usually I will leave directors and producers out of my discussions. This is a "below the line" thing. Actors, writers, directors, and producers are considered "above the line," and all the rest of us working stiffs are "below the line." It is a budget term. It's a handy way to separate the budget into two sections. Oddly enough, the two figures in the budget are pretty equal to one another. Which gives you an idea of how much money those rarefied people take home. Want justice? Buy a gun.

Anyway, the "below-the-line" crew develop a working relationship of sticking together to "get this damn picture done" regardless what the "above-the-liners" do to make our jobs impossible. The harder the picture, the more we have to stick together. Rare is the time when we bond with the "above-the-liners." They have their own circles, and prefer to maintain what we laughingly refer to, but don't really believe, as a "slave-and-massa" relationship.

Despite the obvious line drawn between the above- and below-the-liners, occasionally the line is crossed as with Colla, Hickox, Papazian, and Jay Daniel. These guys are some of my best friends, as they say. We can work together in a professional manner, and play grab-ass at night.

Brian Fuckin' Keith

---

*The secret in singing is found between the
vibration in the singer's voice and the throb
in the hearer's heart.*

—Kahlil Gibran

I WAS JUST FINISHING a truly forgettable movie of the week up in Oregon. We were to wrap the following day, but I was leaving a day early to go home because my dog was sick. Yes, my dog. Jay Daniel, the producer and animal lover himself, thought it a good idea for me to go home.

We were shooting on the coast in Florence, and I had to drive my rental car back to the airport in Eugene. It was a beautiful drive, about an hour and a half, as I recall, through the mountains, and I was looking forward to it.

As I was about to leave, the production manager ran out and asked if I would mind taking Brian Keith along with me. He was one of the stars of the picture, and we had become friendly playing liar's poker in the hotel bar every night. Brian was always good for a laugh and an interesting story, so the trip was stacking up as a nice drive in the country. He was finished with his work also and was anxious to return home.

As we pulled out of the parking lot, Brian asked me why I was leaving a day early. I told him about my poor dog, and he got an even more pained look on his face than he usually had. You'll have to help me here. You'll have to remember what he looked like, and what he sounded like. To say the least, he had a unique delivery, and that delivery was brought forth from a face that seemed to be suffering from an advanced case of constipation. Now, I'm not being unkind. I told him that on numerous occasions as he took my per diem away in the bar every night one dollar at a time.

(Now, oddly enough, I'm not paraphrasing here. I have told this story so often that it is almost a word-for-word recounting from the heart of a kind, good, and sensitive man. He unfolded a very sweet story while looking straight ahead at the Oregon landscape.)

Keith began. "I remember one fuckin' day I was coming out of the fuckin' supermarket, in fuckin' Malibu. There was this fuckin' kid with a fuckin' cardboard box full of the cutest fuckin' puppies you ever fuckin' saw. 'Hey, mister,' the fuckin' kid says, 'You want a free puppy?' Well, I took one of those fuckin' puppies, and took the little fucker fuckin' home.

"Now, I already had a fuckin' dog at home, and the two of them got along fuckin' great. After a couple of fuckin' days, however, I fuckin' realized the fuckin' puppy was fuckin' blind. That's right, fuckin' blind as a fuckin' bat.

"Know what I fuckin' did? I got a fuckin' little fuckin' bell and I put it around my fuckin' dog's fuckin' neck. Little fucker would hear that fuckin' bell and follow the fuckin' dog all over the fuckin' house."

Now he sat back quietly for a few moments, looking at the passing countryside, and appeared to be musing to himself about his infirmed little four-legged friend. After a few minutes he sighed and continued, "You know, Petie, I loved that little fucker. One problem with that fuckin' puppy though: I could never fuckin' housebreak him. The way I fuckin' figured it was he didn't know the fuckin' inside from the fuckin' outside."

How I managed not to wreck the car has always been one of life's great mysteries to me.

Rest in fuckin' peace, Brian Keith.

If We're in Kansas, Someone Should Tell Bob Downey

"Cheshire-puss," she began, "Would you tell me, please, which way I ought to go from here?"

"In that direction," the cat said, waving the right paw round, "lives a hatter; and in that direction," waving the other paw, "lives a March hare. Visit either you like; they're both mad."

"But I don't want to go among mad people," Alice remarked.

"Oh, you can't help that," said the cat; "we're all mad here. I'm mad. You're mad."

"How do you know I'm mad?" said Alice.

"You must be," said the cat, "or you wouldn't have come here."

—Lewis Carroll

IT WAS A SATURDAY NIGHT, and I was sitting in a restaurant up in Ventura County. The waiter informed me that I had a phone call. Who knew I was there? It was the head of production at Warner Brothers. (Some people, it would seem, never learn.) How he knew I was there, I'll never know. The events that followed were so bizarre I never got around to asking.

"Do you know Bob Downey?" Ed Morey asked me. Morey was

the same guy who called me on the stage to meet with Mel Brooks. I said that I knew of him. He was the guy who directed some wacky independent films like *Putney Swope* and *Greaser's Palace*. He was known to be a brick short of a load, but supposedly a great director. "Do us a favor and get on a plane in the morning with Downey and fly to Greenville, North Carolina. You'll be met there by a producer, Danton Risner, whom you don't know, and a production manager, Ira Loonstein, whom you do know. You'll spend the night, look at a military academy Monday, and fly back home Monday night. You have no obligation to do the picture, just look at the location and let them know if it will work. We will messenger you a plane ticket and a script along with Downey's phone number, and you can call him and make arrangements where you'll meet at the airport. We will pay you a lot of money." We have an expression in the business: We all know what we are, we're just haggling over price. Curious whore that I was, how could I say no? What? And give up show business?

"I'm tall, I'll have a gray cap on, and I'll have six Valium in my hand. I'm afraid to fly." That was all I got out of Downey when I called him on the phone. Maybe I jumped into this one a little quickly. What the hell, I didn't have to do the picture, just take an airplane ride.

I walked over to him at the airport and before I spoke I turned his hand over. It was empty. "I already took 'em," slurred Bob. We got on the plane. The attendant asked if we wanted a drink, and he ordered two scotches. We were still on the ground. As we started to taxi he lowered the shade, grabbed the armrest, and slurred, "Are we off the ground yet?" That was the last word he uttered. He passed out with his eyes open, so I took the tray cover they give you in first class and put it over his head. I told the attendant to just pretend he was dead, and settled in to read the script, *Up the Academy*.

In Greenville, after a harrowing plane change in Dallas, I dragged this very tall person up the jetway and delivered him to Risner and Loonstein. We went to a hotel and made arrangements to meet in the coffee shop at eight for breakfast, then go to the military school to make a nine-o'clock appointment.

At eight-thirty, still no Downey. We had been calling his room as well as going up and pounding on the door. No Downey. Fearing the worst, we had hotel security take the door off the hinges. He was sound asleep. We got him up, pulled him together, and off we went to the military school. He was really quite pleasant during all of this, so I was not dreading the day as much as one would expect.

It was an interesting morning. Bob never uttered a word. Usually what happens during such outings is, the director directs. That is, script in hand he looks at the locations and we talk about what should be shot where. He will make suggestions to me as to what he would prefer to do at different spots. But Downey never spoke. So I began to take on his role. "We can play all of scenes 66 through 73 in this spot. I'll build a guard tower over there. A good establishing shot would be from this far corner, and I'll build the building we're going to blow up over there by the football field." I went on like that all morning, and no one was more attentive than Downey. He smiled the whole morning and nodded his agreement.

At one point he came over to me and whispered, yes whispered, in my ear, "Whatever they're paying you isn't enough."

At lunch, Downey was absolutely charming. He was animated, and he spoke of many things. Except we never talked about the picture. That's okay; he was cute, and we laughed a lot and had a pleasant lunch. I never had the opportunity to ask the other guys if they thought there was anything strange about the way the day was going.

Back at the school, the afternoon was a repeat of the morning. Me playing director, and Bob smiling and nodding a lot.

At the airport Bob said to the ticket agent, "I want to sit in the no dying section, or just put me beside the nuns and babies. God doesn't kill nuns and babies." And we all got on the plane, Downey and Loonstein in 2A and 2B and Risner and I in 3A and 3B. We were flying along and, thank God, there was hardly anyone else in first class. Dan turned to me and said, "What do you think of my director?" At that precise moment Bob passed a lit joint over the back of his seat to us. As calmly as I could I said, "If he were my director, I would fire his ass."

The rest of the flight went calmly enough, and I got home without further incident. That's the last I'll ever hear from Bob Downey, I mused.

About two days later I got a call from Robert Shapiro, who was head of worldwide, yes worldwide, production for the Brothers Warner. "Peter, would you mind stopping by my office tomorrow morning at nine for a cup of coffee?" Now, I don't get that kind of invitation every day. As a matter of fact, there was simply no reason to believe Shapiro even knew who I was. Here was another invitation I found impossible to ignore. I suspected it had something with the Downey episode, and I was feeling very much like Alice falling down the rabbit hole.

Promptly at nine I strolled through the door and into an office that could have served as a sound stage. It was so big it echoed.

This is a part of Hollywood that hairy-legged production designers don't normally frolic in. My office across the lot was about the size of Shapiro's coffee table. I was greeted warmly by "call me Bob" Shapiro, Danton Risner, Ira Loonstein, and, you guessed it, Bob Downey. The pleasantries were gotten out of the way, the coffee was sipped, and Shapiro turned to me with a grin and asked, "Peter, what do you think of my director?" I flashed back to the airplane, looked at Downey, and expected him to hand me a joint. Downey was sitting in front of a window flooded with early-morning light, rendering him back-lit and in silhouette; no face. I placed my cup gently back on its saucer and slowly sat back. I looked into the black hole which was Downey and said directly to him, "Bob, I'll tell you what I told your producer on the plane the other night: If you were my director, I would fire your ass."

We have all heard the expression "pregnant silence." Well, this silence was just plain knocked up. There was a subtle clearing of throats and coffee cups were placed silently onto saucers. Finally, Shapiro spoke. "Gentlemen, would you mind waiting outside for a few minutes?" He was referring to Risner, Loonstein and me, leaving himself and Downey alone. We all walked to the outer office and went into separate corners and stood there staring into those corners. Silence. I thought I had really fallen down the rabbit hole, and whatever I had left in the sane world, I would never again see. Minutes slogged by. Silence.

Suddenly the door flew open and out ran Downey with a big smile on his face, heading straight for me. "I just told this asshole I wouldn't do his fucking picture if you wouldn't do it with me, you beautiful son of a bitch!"

We ended up doing the picture in Salina, Kansas, at St. John's Military School. Bob Downey never did find that brick to make a full load, and I'm sure they are still talking about him back there. Rest assured, however, that whatever they are saying, it is kind and they are smiling.

POSTSCRIPT: While we were shooting, Downey's preteen son played with his motorscooter in the hotel parking lot, showing not the slightest interest in what we were doing. A few years later, that same kid got an Academy Award nomination for a brilliant performance as "Chaplin." And oh, yes, I still have no idea what the hell that meeting was all about in Shapiro's office. In the infinite wisdom of Warner Brothers, they hired another producer, Marvin Worth, who insisted that every night after we wrapped, Ira Loonstein, Dan Risner, he, and I meet in Downey's suite and, page by page, go over the next day's shooting schedule. At these nightly meetings, Downey never said a word except, "Anyone want a drink?"

Man, I Feel Like John Wayne

*It always seems to me that so few people
live—they just seem to exist—and I don't
see any reason why we shouldn't live
always—till we die physically, why do we
do it all in our teens and twenties?*
—*Georgia O'Keeffe*

WHEN THEY MADE *The Wizard of Oz* in 1938 the antics of
the little people hired to portray the Munchkins became the stuff
of legend. When you get three or four little people in a room—
especially a bar—God knows what will happen. Put 125 of them in
a room, especially a bar, and insanity reins. We did a movie back in
the eighties called *Under the Rainbow*. It told the story of the making of *The Wizard of Oz* with a couple of side stories to round it all
out. It starred Chevy Chase, Carrie Fisher, Eve Arden, Billy Barty,
the always elegant Joe Maher, and the ever-lovin' Pat McCormick.
And 125 little people. The reason for the movie was that if one
little person was funny, 125 of them would be a hoot. Wrong.
When the script called for all of them to run across the hotel
lobby, we didn't know that you had to time them with a calendar.
As in comedy, in which timing is everything, it just wasn't working. We had a good script, wonderful actors, and, if I do say so
myself, damn good sets. It just wasn't funny. The director had
never directed comedy before, and he was a little wanting when it

Who knew Carrie Fisher would become such a brilliant writer?

came to constructing both the joke and the reaction to the joke (something quite essential).

The little people did leave me with many memories. To put it mildly, I ain't a big guy, but they made me feel like one. One morning we were preparing to shoot. It was very foggy, and the little people had on their Munchkin costumes. All those bright colors and ruffles and those high voices made them seem like a garden of human flowers. There I was, standing in the middle of all of them. They were moving about and talking, and I was towering over them. I really did feel like John Wayne in a garden.

After work, back at their hotel, they were attempting to recreate the 1938 antics. It really was a hoot to show up there. Most of them were standing on the bar. That way, you see, they could look the standard-size customers sitting at the bar right in the eye. There was always, it seemed, a laundry basket full of them careening down one of the halls propelled by two or three pushers, with beer bottles flying and whisky bottles gripped in tiny little mitts.

It ain't easy being a little person. You aren't expected to live long, and life is pretty painful. Joints aren't very kind, and your insides are not always where they are supposed to be. I had the construction crew make a lot of two-steps so they could easily negotiate the urinals. For the salad bar at lunch time, I had a ramp built so they could reach the different salads. About halfway through shooting, however, they were back on the floor on one side of the salad bar, and the regular-sized crew was on the other side on the ramp bending waaaay down.

Okay, it wasn't a very good film, but it was a love-fest. We had, at the time, the littlest person in the world. He was a touch less than three feet tall. In real life, when we found him, he was a dispatcher for the Youngstown, Ohio, sheriff's department. He had no thoughts of show biz, but he came to California at Billy Barty's urging. I was always so afraid he was going to fall off or tip his chair over at lunchtime, so I designed and had built a tall chair for him so that he could eat sitting instead of kneeling. It was a round chair with a spiral staircase. When he came in to lunch the day it was finished, we escorted him to his new seat. He walked around it a couple times and announced, "I need a fucking seat belt."

I was asked to play a part in the film. I played the director of *Gone with the Wind*, Victor Flemming. I had one line, which I pushed into three or four. They asked me how much I wanted to play the part. I told them that I wanted a dressing room one foot longer than Chevy Chase's. They obliged. They got me a truck. Ben Massi had painted on the sides in large letters, "Peter Wooley's upstairs dressing room." They put an old mud-splattered mattress in there, along with an old Warner Brothers back-lot dressing table strapped to the inside of the truck. They put lace over the back opening, and attached a ramp I could walk up. Then, for reasons I'll never be able to explain, they put a large throne-like chair facing the back where I could sit and look out.

The director and his wife celebrated their tenth wedding anniversary while we were shooting. By tradition, the tenth anniversary should be celebrated by gifts of tin. (Don't ask me who came up with that one.) In keeping with the spirit of the picture, it was

"Step right up, have your tickets ready!
Hey, little shaver..."

decided that I would dress in the Tin Man outfit and present them with roses at some moment during the shooting day. The make-up department got some silver face make-up, and the costume department found the Tin Man suit, and I was appropriately attired. At a proper minute, I presented them with their flowers, and all was well.

Maybe not all was well. There I was dressed up like Ray Bolger. The little ceremony didn't seem to be enough for getting dressed up like that and then taking it all off. Linda, who was coming home that night from a business trip, was expecting me to pick her up at the Burbank airport. Perfect. I would pick her up as the Tin Man. I commandeered my "dressing room," sat on my throne, and, with a gang of friends, went to pick up Linda.

Those humorless bastards at the airport wouldn't let me through the metal detector, but I greeted her, nonetheless, sitting on my throne. All of us went dancing at a bar in Burbank. God bless Linda. Verbally or in print I have said that a jillion times: God bless Linda.

The only hat I ever had that fit properly,
but I look to be a quart low.

Tracy

*It's not true that nice guys finish last. Nice
guys are winners before the game even
starts.*

—*Addison Walker*

WHEN TRACY BOUSMAN and I went onto the Paramount
lot to do the first year of "Mod Squad," we couldn't stand the
thought of moving into yet another studio art department. We began to search around the lot for some clandestine place to set up
an office. Behind the commissary on the Desilu side of the lot was
a two-story structure known as the directors building. The second
floor was full of offices, including the Mod Squad production
office. The first floor had been used for storage for so long that
people no longer knew or cared what was, in fact, stored therein.
Tracy and I broke in and moved all the stuff to the back half of the
building. We changed the locks, and arranged for our construction
crew to build us a rather pleasant suite. We went to the prop house
with our set decorator, Ned Parsons, and pulled furniture out of
there to decorate our place like a Joan Crawford movie. We had
phones installed because the phone company didn't ask questions,
and we listed ourselves on the Paramount Studio directory. One
day I saw a stuffed eight-foot gorilla being rolled down the street.
I thought to myself, what a great thing to have in the entry of the
office. As it got closer, I saw that Tracy was pushing it. When he

saw me, he grinned, "Won't this look great in the office entry?" He would never tell me how or where he got it, not that I gave a damn. It stood in the entry all the time we were there with a script in one hand and a cigarette in the other wearing a "Mod Squad" hat.

My office was furnished with a nine-foot-long green crushed velvet couch, a glass coffee table, an inflatable chair (they were the coolest in the sixties), a game table with four chairs, and a bar I'm sure I saw in a Joan Crawford movie. When you lifted the top, the contents rose from the interior like Atlantis from the ocean. No drawing table, desk, or other professional, workmanlike device was to be seen. Actually, all those accoutrements were secreted away in a back room, away from prying eyes. I did a lot of work in that back room, but no one saw me doing it. It seemed important to both Tracy and me that the perception was we didn't do anything. It all just seemed to happen like a duck swimming. All seemed calm above water, but the feet were going like hell beneath it.

With great ceremony we installed a sign at our new front door. We were in business.

Danny Thomas was coming onto the lot to begin preparation for "Make Room For Grandaddy." (The show I was going to do, but didn't know it, two seasons later.) As was Paramount's practice then, they bought him a new golf cart to get around the lot. They bought golf carts for everyone who didn't need them. Danny's office was next door to the stage he would eventually use. If people wanted to see Danny, they came to him. The commissary (right across the street) delivered his lunch. He not only didn't need a cart, he didn't know he had one. Tracy and I "liberated" it, pried off Danny's name tag and had the cart repainted. I sent Paramount operations a thank-you note on Danny's stationery. We stayed in that office and drove that golf cart for more than three years, and no one at the studio ever mentioned it. To this day, I still don't think they had a clue.

The other day I was over at Paramount and I went by to see our old place. The whole first floor has been redesigned into legit offices, and our Joan Crawford movie was nowhere to be found.

Tracy Bousman Died

Written as an obituary in the
Art Directors' Newsletter

IT WAS RAINING like a son of a bitch. The water pounded the New York pavement with such intensity that it looked out of focus. I had just left the Guggenheim Museum and decided to walk back to 55th Street. Two blocks later, it started. It was a warm rain, so, what the hell, what's the big deal? I started to whistle and, feeling a little like Gene Kelly, I got happily and musically wet.

When I got back to the hotel, I ran into the room laughing and singing. "Tracy died," my wife cried. It was the longest fall I ever took. Tracy Bousman had been my friend for almost forty years. I had met him when we were both working in the same architectural office. He had introduced me to the "movie business," and when I decided that that was what I wanted to do the rest of my life, he had made it happen. He had made me an assistant art director a few years later, and had put me in line to get my own show a year after that. He had been my professional and spiritual adviser during all those years. Tracy and his wife, Elizabeth, had even been our neighbors for five years when we shared a duplex in Hancock Park. We made avant-garde 8-mm movies on the weekends with Walter Herndon and my son, Chris. I had once knocked on their door naked on Halloween.

After fighting a number of complications for three months at

Tracy Bousman and John Solie having a laugh on me.

UCLA, Tracy Bousman has moved on. He leaves a body of work in his paintings, drawings, and sketches that will hopefully make someone rich someday. While he was in the hospital, we talked about making a video of his work set to music, the perfect thing to play at parties or just as a respite from regular television offerings. He was the classic 'forties and 'fifties painter. Two of his early pieces hang in my daughter's house. He was able to show his humor, as well as his sadness, every time he put pencil or brush to a flat surface.

Tracy had a unique history. He was a member of the last mounted cavalry unit in the U.S. Army. He turned in his horse in Australia, and stayed in the Pacific the whole of World War II under serious combat conditions. He could whip anything but his own body. After the war he returned to the United States and taught art at Chouinard Art Institute. He played the violin, mandolin, and beat the hell out of the drums. For a time he sold Bibles, gathering crowds by playing the fiddle. Before his retirement in 1997, he was a member of 876 for 32 years. His credits include such television series as "Mod Squad," "Spencer for Hire," and "Young Riders." He was seventy-nine years old.

His loving wife of forty-seven years, Elizabeth, a daughter, Claudia, and three sisters, Mary, Lura, and Jeanne, survive him. And me.

No services are currently scheduled, but a "wrap party" is being planned. Elizabeth will scatter his ashes in the Pacific he defended and loved.

Yesterdays

WHEN I WAS A SET DESIGNER at Warners in the mid-sixties, the drafting room was long and narrow, with two rows of drafting tables, about fifteen to a row, running front to back. There was always a lot of crosstalk and joke-telling going on. There was an old guy named Fred Stoos who retired during that time who would make up dirty limericks as he worked. When he had one done to his satisfaction, he would write it down and come back to my drawing board and read it to me. He liked me, I guess, because I was the youngest person in the department and he was the old-est. I was unquestionably his best audience. As a matter of fact, when he retired he gave me a book, which I still have, that con-tained things he had written down during all his years in the busi-ness. It was full of things he had deemed important and wanted to save. Things like the minimum turning radius of a train or the dis-tance from the sun to all the planets in our solar system. There were jokes and cartoons, mathematical equations, and even a pho-tograph of two circus elephants mating.

A group of us went to lunch together every day. There was never a shortage of good restaurants around Warners, so lunch-time usually became a raucous-and-wet affair. We could pack more insanity into one hour than people are expected or encouraged to do. One day, when it was time to go back to work, I was having entirely too much fun to leave right away. The boys left me at the bar.

An hour later I sauntered back into the drafting room trying to look casual, as if I had just been to the restroom. I walked to my drafting table. It wasn't there. My bench, along with all my personal belongings and equipment, was also gone. Even the space I had once occupied seemed to be missing! Everyone had his head down and was drawing away, not even looking at me, or so it seemed. Suddenly I felt as though I were invisible. I stood there and looked at the space I had once occupied that no longer existed. Very "Twilight Zone."

Of course I figured out what they had done to me: They had simply carried all my stuff out of the room, and rearranged their places so that I no longer had a presence. They were all ignoring me as if I wasn't there, and I couldn't let the bastards get away with it. Since my place was gone and I was invisible, I made an elaborate show of cartoon tiptoeing the long way out of the room so everyone could see me, and I went home.

The next morning when I came in, my place had miraculously returned.

We had sort of an unofficial club at Warners that met every Thursday evening after work. Payday in the movie business has always been Thursday and that determined the meeting day of the SHIT Club. "Shit," of course, stood for "Sure Happy It's Thursday." Our meetings were held in one local tavern or another, and we never discussed anything of importance. Actually, that was the only club rule we had; never, ever, discuss anything of any social, artistic, political, or religious value. Bragging, lying, joke-telling, insulting, and gossiping were about all that was permitted. Three of those guys are now retired, two are dead, one of them has just disappeared, and I am the only one still around making noise.

In the mid-sixties, Ward Preston and I were "farmed out" on a temporary basis from Warner Brothers to Universal. That assured Stan Fleischer, department head at Warners, that he could get us back whenever he needed us. It was always amazing to me that anyone would want us back but, truth be told, we were both very good at what we did.

One day, Preston was on the back lot, and his drafting board was right in front of mine. I happened to notice a very large box over by the coffee machine. I went over, got the box and put it on his board. I wrote a card that said, "Take this home to your wife." I got in the box and had the guys tape it shut with the card on top. And I waited.

Eventually, he came back, read the note, and set the box on fire. It got deathly quiet in the drafting room for a few minutes until the smoke and flames began to filter into the box. I came out of there like a stripper out of a cake, accompanied by hoots and hollers from the entire art department, who had come in to the drafting room to witness the spectacle. The next day part of the back lot burned down, and everyone was sure I did it. In my defense, I reminded them that Ward was the one who had set fire to the box.

I never did fit into the corporate image at Universal. They were always so uptight and straight-laced. I put a rather large sign in one of the drafting room windows that read, "Support Mental Health Or I'll Kill You." The way they acted, you would have thought I used dirty words.

Life, Like Shit, Happens

We'll have early morning madness
We'll have magic in the making…
  —*"Sunset Boulevard,"*
  lyrics by Don Black &
  Christopher Hampton

IT ISN'T HEALTHY to get up in the morning when it is still dark. You start by pushing from your body a very large bag of fear, and you try to set it aside for a moment so it doesn't get wet while you shave and shower.

You drive your car to a large building known as a sound stage, or to a location where there are many trucks parked in front with many people doing serious things and frowning a lot. You park, get out of your car, get back in your car and park it someplace else because some production assistant, who thinks his job depends on it, insists you park some place else because you're "in the shot," and you know the shot and you're not in it.

You move your car because the kid's job is indeed on the line, and you search for the camera because you know the director and cameraman can't be too far away. You find the director, who is trying to eat a breakfast sandwich, drink a cup of coffee, and keep ten people at bay so he can get his first shot as soon as possible so he can look good on the production report. He usually looks like he has taken a cup of hemlock, but the studio won't allow him to die.

He sees you, begins discussing yesterday's fuck-ups as if there were anything you or anyone else could do about them. This is the precise moment the cameraman sees you and informs you he can't light the set because of that big overhang. Never mind that he saw your sketches, watched it being built, and last week on the tech scout he talked to his gaffer and grip about the best way to light it. Everyone was full of praise about how neat the set looked. The cameraman is usually the one who administers the hemlock to the director. The producer is standing nearby, if it isn't too early, reciting the producer mantra, "You're not dead until I tell you you're dead."

Being away from home and hearth for long periods of time is not an easy thing to survive. Relationships are constantly being tested. Artistic integrity is difficult to maintain when there are so many outside demons trying to sabotage it: Not enough time. Not enough money. It's raining. It's snowing. The star has an ingrown toenail and won't come out of his or her trailer. The wardrobe department fit the actress in a red dress, ignoring the color palate I gave them two months ago, so I will have to repaint a set so the actress doesn't disappear. The director picked a new camera angle at the last minute, and there is a wall in the way. The producer's wife, who has been hit upside the head too many times with *Architectural Digest*, doesn't like the couch, and thinks I should fire my decorator. The director of photography, who has seen the location at least five hundred times in the last two months, has decided at the eleventh hour that he can't light it. The production manager has just informed me that my budget has been cut yet again because the star's agent just called and informed him that according to his or her contract, his or her trailer is not nearly large enough. And there is always that fear thing. I have never talked to anyone in this business, executive, star, or director, who has not admitted to the fear. We are all afraid of failing in one way or another, and we are all afraid that someone is going to "find us out" and expose us for the frauds we see ourselves to be. Well, you get the picture. This business is not for the faint of heart, just the special.

This scene does not change much from picture to picture or

"Looks fine to me—shoot it."

from day to day. Sometimes there is a smile or two. Sometimes there is a scream or two. Always there is a sort of electricity.

I'm convinced that there is a bit of magic in this early-morning chaos. Out of this, more often than not, comes art. What is happening here is something an efficiency "expert" could not tolerate, but we're making movies, not widgets. Let's face it, there is magic going on. And in those mornings when fear kicks in, and I feel the panic of not having enough talent or ability to get through the day, I force myself to stop and ask, "What! And give up show business?"

Like all rules, there are exceptions. Richard Colla, for one. He makes magic by going through another sort of ritual. He insists that we play, and, by the time we are face to face on the set in the morning, we will talk about any damn thing to keep from getting bogged down in the angst racket. Bryan Hickox is another. As a producer, he carries cheer with him wherever he goes. He produced, Richard Colla directed, and I designed a pilot for 20th Century Fox called "Jake's Way." It was joy to the world every day. Of course it didn't sell, so maybe some suffering is called for. Just count me out.

Carl Reiner is another of those old-fashioned guys who has done it all and just refuses to get excited. I did one picture with him, a John Candy starrer, *Summer Rental*, and Reiner was a joy. He never asked me back to do another, however, and that has always perplexed me.

The late Hal Ashby signed a two-picture back-to-back deal with Lorimar and couldn't use his regular production designer on either of them because of time constraints, so he asked me to do the first one. The original title was *The Hamster of Happiness* and it became *Second Hand Hearts* by release date. It was the best dialogue I ever read in a script, and I was thrilled to be working with the director of *Harold and Maude* and *Shampoo*. What I didn't know was that he was a truly troubled soul. He actually said to me once that he really didn't like anything I was doing on the picture, but he'd go ahead and shoot it anyway. Chuck Mulvehill, the line producer, kept shoring me up by telling me Hal didn't like much of anything at all, and I should just keep going. It was all looking great. Haskell Wexler, the great cinematographer, was shooting it, and he repeated Mulvehill's advice, but still every day was a bummer. Robert Blake and Barbara Harris were starring in the picture, and they were running amok, but Ashby didn't seem to care. He had one foot out the door from the beginning, wanting to get to *Being There*. That was the second picture in his deal, and he really loved the script. When we finished *Hamster*, he threw it in the corner, went off and did *Being There*, cut, released it, then went back and edited *Hamster*. So I had the honor of doing his only real flop, and suffering for the privilege. Haskell did say nice things about me in an interview for an article in *American Cinematographer Magazine*. That picture represented the beginning of the end of "fun" in the film business. One last thought: Years before I had worked as a set designer on *Torn Curtain*, directed by the legendary Alfred Hitchcock. He was famous for the way he intimidated actresses. He is quoted as saying, "I never, ever, said actors are like cattle. What I said was, 'Actors should be treated like cattle.'" Barbara Harris had just finished *Family Plot* for Hitch, and she was such a flake that I was curious how she got on with him.

"Funny you should ask," Barbara said, "My first day of shooting, I came out of make-up and walked onto the set and positioned myself in front of Mr. Hitchcock so that he could give me any direction he wished to give me before we started shooting. He was sitting in his chair reading the *London Times* and not paying any attention to the lighting preparation, and certainly not paying any mind to me. Finally, after five minutes, I sort of cleared my throat, and spoke through the newspaper. 'Mr. Hitchcock, is there anything you would like to tell me before we start?'

"He slowly lowered the paper and stared at me for a moment. Then he said in his best Alfred Hitchcock impression, 'Yes. Know what to say and where to stand.'"

I was never so happy to see a picture end as I was that one. I always felt like I was marching out of step. Hell, maybe I was.

I did the aforementioned "Jake's Way" right after that and managed to keep the "fun" a little longer. Of course that was with Hickox and Colla, and all the stops got pulled. We had scheduled a funeral sequence, and I found this wonderful cemetery outside of New Bronfells, Texas, with a classic white clapboard church in the middle of it. I arranged to have us there early in the morning so that the church and the scene itself could be shot in back light. We got some fog machines to lay a layer of ground fog over the scene. Then, without telling anyone, I got a half-dozen sheep to graze in the background among the tombstones. Also without telling anyone, I got some lipstick and painted big red lips on one of the sheep. I called her Ethel, and we developed a relationship during her time in make-up. The scene was lovely. Neither Colla nor Hickox saw the lips until they were in the editing room after shooting ended. They were cutting in New York for some reason or other, and went over to F.A.O. Schwartz during a break. A few days later, I received in the mail a life-size stuffed sheep with red lips and a note that said, "Remember me? Love, Ethel." Can you imagine those two clowns standing in the toy store putting lips on that sheep? Oh, I almost forgot. When you lifted her tail, there was a little door you could open, and a little baby lamb slid out.

During a later shooting for the same film in Bandera, Texas,

Colla, Hickox, and me.
Every deck should have three jokers.

the company was staying at a dude ranch about three miles from
our main location, which was a large, elegant ranch on which were
a great number of exotic and beautiful animals. I arranged for
Colla and me to take over the guesthouse on the ranch. It had a
living room, dining room, and kitchen, and on either side were
wonderful guest suites. We would get up in the morning, make a
pot of coffee, and wander outside in our bathrobes to greet the
company, who were arriving by bus from the dude ranch. Mean-
while the ranch hands would have saddled a couple of horses for
us and tied them to a cast-iron white guy in our front yard. We
would walk over to an adjacent fence, say hello to a few camels
that were looking for a handout, climb on our gallant steeds, and
go to work. In short, we were in cowboy heaven.

Actually, that's where I really learned to ride. Slim Pickins, with whom I had gotten friendly on *Blazing Saddles,* was also on the picture. Pickins, an old rodeo rider and clown, was an excellent horseman. He actually got his name when he first went into rodeoing. He was just a kid, and his parents didn't want him to participate in such a sport, so he did it on the sly. The old cowboys told him his chance of winning anything was pretty slim, and to protect his anonymity from his parents, named him Slim Pickins. It stuck, and the rest is history. I don't even know his real name. Anyway, one day as we were waiting around to get a shot, I asked him if he would give me a few pointers. He had me get up on his horse, which was so tall that you risked a nosebleed sitting on him. "Get your ass in the back of that saddle," Pickins instructed. "That will keep your heels down. Talk to the big bastard with the inside of your legs. If he don't do what you want, get off, go around front and punch the bastard in the nose." End of instruction. Slim Pickins was one of the sweetest men to ever stand in front of a camera. Look in the dictionary under "sincere" and I'm sure you'll find Slim's picture.

At the end of the workday, the company would get on the bus and return to the dude ranch. Colla and I would ride our horses over there, and have dinner with everyone. Then, after a few after-dinner drinks, we would allow the horses to find their way home with us sitting there trying to look like cowboys.

One day I had to go into town for some sort of meeting, so I drove my rental car. On the far side of Bandera I passed a big old roadhouse called the Longbranch Saloon. "Peter," I said, "you may never pass this way again. You may never again in your life have the opportunity to ride a horse up to a place called the Long-branch Saloon." The next evening after dinner, I announced my intentions to Colla. He thought that was probably the worst idea I ever had. With his arm around the leading lady, he suggested I go it alone. I went it alone. I stopped for all the stoplights through town and pulled that beauty up to the saloon. There was no hitching rail, so I tied him to the bumper of a pick-up truck at the front door.

I walked in, sat at the bar, ordered a beer, and challenged some local to a game of pool. I had a great evening getting to know all of Bandera's best. Some hours later, a nice man came over and asked, "That your horse out front?"

"Yes sir, I expect it is. What can I do for you?" Trying to sound "local."

"You got it tied to my pick-up, and I gotta git on home." We walked out together, and I untied my trusty steed. "Mighty good piece of horse flesh you got there."

"To tell you the truth, sir, this steed belongs to my host, who is letting me use it while I'm in town. I can make him go and stop. I can even make him run like the wind. But I know nothing about, as you say, 'horse flesh.' As a matter of fact, I have not yet been able to locate the radio or the heater."

Ignoring my rapier-like repartee, he suggested, "We still steal horses here, and that beauty is in the range of fifty thousand bucks. If I were you, I wouldn't leave him unattended. Have a nice evenin'."

I am truly nuts, but I'm not stupid. I went back in, paid my bill, said "Adios" to my new best friends, and saddled up. I rode across the street to a convenience store, bought a six pack, opened one and hung the other five from my saddle horn by the plastic thingy that holds the cans all together. I started back through town. It was summer, so it was still light outside, and I dutifully stopped at all the stoplights. At one light a police car pulled up alongside me. The officer in the passenger seat looked up at me on my trusty stallion, and the driver bent down so he could look up and witness this sight.

"How ya doin'?" asked the closest officer.

"Better'n average," I announced, patting the sturdy neck of my charge and taking an elegant sip of my Lone Star Beer.

"You headed directly, I mean directly, back to the ranch, cowboy?"

"Truly I am, sir." I grinned.

"Have a pleasant evening." The light changed, and I rode on. Obviously I had missed a drunken riding charge by a hair.

You know those cute little miniature horses, the ones that look so cuddly? Forget it. Colla and I stayed an extra day after we wrapped so we could explore the whole ranch and all its exotic inhabitants. We had a great day, and when we were headed back to the house by another route, we opened the gate and went into an apparently empty field. I closed the gate, got back up, and we headed along, little dogie. A low thundering sound began to rise from the trees to our left. Out of the trees came at least one hundred miniature horses. Pissed off, for some reason. We probably could have outrun them, but it was such a strange sight we never thought of that. We did keep moving, however, but they literally attacked us. I had to kick them away to keep them from biting my legs, and they kept trying to bite the underside of our steeds' necks. It was a harrowing ride to the gate on the other side of the field, which had to be unlatched and opened. Richard did the honors while I rode back and forth kicking at the bastards to keep them at bay. We truly escaped, because they were intent on our death. They're mean bastards, and what good are they? You can't ride 'em. I put them in the same category as lions, tigers, bears, and asps.

After all these years, Hickox and Colla still think I'm carrying on an affair with that sheep. I can honestly tell you that Ethel and I have not communicated in any way for some time now.

Creative Insanity

HE WAS LYING in the middle of Forest Lawn Drive in the rain, waiting for me with a smile on his face. At the time, I was in bed with his wife, waiting for him with a smile on *my* face.

John Solie has been a fellow traveler in that space, just out of reach of the normal and serious-minded, we have always referred to as creative insanity. When we are together we never have a serious conversation, unless, of course, one of us really needs it. This sort of relationship has kept us in good stead for over thirty years.

Early in our friendship we were both working on different projects at Warner Brothers, and he invited me over to his house in Glendale one evening after work. He gave me explicit instructions on how to get there, since I had not yet been to his house. We left Warners about the same time, Solie a minute before.

He went right to Forest Lawn Drive, the first leg of his instructions, and I went another direction. Thus I arrived at his house before him, while he was lying in the middle of the street. His wife Shirley met me at the door, and I said, "Quick, let's get into bed before John gets home!"

When Solie had been almost run over a couple of times and was soaking wet and muddy, he lost interest and went home.

When he arrived, he wandered through the house looking for me after seeing my car out front. He finally got to the bedroom to find Shirley and me under the covers. I couldn't wait to get his reaction.

"Do you have any idea how long I've been lying in the rain waiting for you?" he screamed. He ranted and raved and completely ignored the fact that we were supposedly involved in love-making.

To shut him up, I said from deep under the covers, "Can this wait? It must be obvious to you that we're very busy. Please leave." He left.

John Solie is a very talented artist and illustrator. He has done at least a dozen *TV Guide* covers, as well as covers for the now-defunct *Saturday Evening Post*. (I blame him for its demise.) In recent years he has done the covers of paperback books and countless portraits of people, famous and not so famous. He did a portrait of Linda that hangs in our dining room. Shirley is a super-beautiful lady, both inside and out, and, along with Linda, manages to keep up as John and I travel through creative insanity.

Over the years I have had occasion to hire Solie to do portraits needed for projects I was working on. Each time brought with it an outrageous story.

The first project we worked on together was *Blazing Saddles*. He did two portraits. One was a front view of Harvey Korman dressed as a groom, standing next to the ugliest bride Solie could paint. The other was a rear view of the same portrait. The front view hung in Governor Le Petomane's (Mel Brooks) office over the fireplace. The rear view was in Headley Lamarr's (Harvey Korman) office, which was next to the governor's office, above a back-to-back fireplace. Korman could stand on a chair and, after adjusting the portrait, substitute his entire face and spy into the Governor's office. Sadly, the portrait was taken out of the final cut of the film. However, it was enough to get our relationship under way.

Warners sent me over to Honolulu for a long weekend to look in on the beginning of a new season of "The Brain Keith Show." That was before I knew him as Brian Fuckin' Keith. I mentioned to Solie that I was going to Hawaii for the weekend. When I got on the plane he was sitting there. I mustered up all my presence of mind and managed to walk past him to my seat without acknowledging him.

When the seatbelt sign went off, Solie, beside himself, came back to my seat and said, "I'm staying with you in Honolulu."

I turned to the stranger sitting next to me and asked, "Is he talking to you? I don't know this guy." Solie stood there for a few minutes longer while I ignored him, then went back to his seat. I did not even speak to him until we were well inside the Honolulu terminal. We had a great weekend.

I was doing an ABC movie of the week, and I needed a nude portrait of Doug McClure. Obviously, it was a rear view. Enter Solie. We went to McClure and had him take his shirt off and strike a rear-view pose. Solie went to work on the portrait.

One evening he called me and asked if I could come over and pose for him for a few minutes because he was having trouble getting the back muscles right. Of course I went over and hit the pose with my shirt off, and Solie went to work. He is a very fast painter, but he seemed to be taking forever. When I finally began to complain, he jumped up and announced that he was finished. Sure enough, he had Doug McClure's back muscles perfectly painted. He had also done a portrait of a Ruebenesque cherub. A gay Ruebenesque cherub who looked exactly like me. It hangs in my office, and I cherish it.

One season I was asked to design the last four shows of "The Streets of San Francisco." I required a life-sized portrait in one of the sets that shot first thing the following Monday morning. It was Thursday when I called Solie to come to San Francisco and save us.

When he arrived I gave him the bad news that the actress in the portrait had not yet been cast. She would be cast before Monday morning. That was all I knew. Casting would call my hotel and let us know who it was and when she would arrive. In the meantime we were told to have a good weekend.

Neither Solie nor I are what you could call easily panicked.

Even a production designer has a little ham in him.

We decided on a pose, and found a dress we liked in the wardrobe department. I put the dress on, hit the pose, and Solie painted the whole portrait except the face. We picked jewelry from a glamor magazine, and he even painted that into the picture.

We then had a crazy San Francisco weekend. We laughed all weekend at how easy it would be to paint in my ugly face, along with ersatz breasts, and be sitting on a masterpiece. It would be as though Oscar Wilde had written Dorian Gray as a woman whose face turned into mine.

The actress—for the life of me, I can't remember her name—arrived at the hotel at four o'clock on Sunday afternoon. We met her in the hotel bar. She and Solie got appropriately sloshed, then retired to his room to get to work. When I opened my hotel room door on Monday morning there stood a magnificent painting ready for hanging. Of course the paint was still wet, but the camera never knew.

Solie called me one afternoon and said he had to paint a portrait of actor Richard Anderson along with a fictitious family of a wife, son, and daughter the same ages as my wife and kids. He said, "Let me use Linda and the kids in the portrait. Then, after they're finished with it, I'll paint you into the picture and you'll have a nice family portrait."

It sounded like a good deal to me, so Solie painted away. But Anderson liked the damn thing so well he insisted on keeping it for himself. Someplace in this town is a family portrait of Richard Anderson and my family. More's the pity.

At my sixtieth birthday party at the Half Moon Saloon in Big Sky, Montana, Solie grabbed the microphone and made the following speech:

"Peter and I have a friendship that goes back a long time. We've had, and I'm not ashamed to say, a deep love for one another that has lasted almost twenty-five years. For eighteen years Peter has found me to be one of the finest, kindest, most loving, and attractive men he has ever known, and for the first seven years I liked him okay too. Now, today I would put those twenty-five years up against any eight-month period I have witnessed or been a party to in the last six and a half years.

"Peter is, in my estimation, and shall continue to be, for all intents and purposes, one of, if not the only, in all candor, and I speak not only for myself, but for anyone and everyone who should or would prefer now or at any other time in their lives to penetrate or otherwise engage in, whether it be piercing or informal, one of the most intelligent, well behaved, and, last but not least, silent witnesses.

"All of which brings me to the time Peter got his dick caught in a potato peeler." Then he sat down.

The Solies moved up to Oregon, where he has become a gentleman portrait artist. We talk nonsense on the phone about every other week. They live in a hundred-year-old house on a windswept bluff overlooking the ocean. John thinks he's Heathcliff, and Shirley thinks he's nuts.

Also Dead

All men are not creative equally.
                                                   —John Solie

IMAGINE THIS: You're flying in a single-engine airplane. At night. In a fierce rain and thunderstorm. The pilot is thin-lipped and holding on with both hands. In the plane is a producer, a production manager, the pilot, you, and a world-famous director.

The airplane is struck by lightning and crashes. You all die.

The next day all the news services are screaming, "World-famous director killed in plane crash." They go on to tell about the single-engine plane going down in a major storm and rescuers having a difficult time getting to the wreckage in the mountains. They then tell about the movie the famous director was preparing and who was to be starring in it. They offer a sad quote from a famous movie star. The next six paragraphs are devoted to all the wonderful films the famous director has done, and all the good and philanthropic deeds he has performed. They mention how well his grieving widow is holding up, and quote her. The head of the studio shows up for the television cameras in an open-collared shirt, looking haggard and pretending to be on the verge of tears. (Not just the actors are actors in this town.)

After the press has exhausted all the avenues of grief and pain, the last paragraph will begin with the words, "Also dead...."

Please understand that this is not something I imagine. I have seen this sort of thing on many occasions. It performs two very bad functions. First, it gives famous people a much larger sense of their own importance. They are human beings, after all, and they can't help but think, "That could have been me." As soon as they are finished writing their own obituaries, and embellishing the hell out of them, they start to miss themselves.

Second, and just as tragically, it diminishes our own self-worth. If famous people had their way, they would slam the door on anyone else who wished to join their ranks. "There are enough famous people already!" In that they may have a point. In fact, there are certainly too many. You could have a list of credits and awards as long as the proverbial arm, but if you ain't famous, you ain't shit.

I must say, my first brush with famous personages was a pleasant and lasting experience. My first project as a full art director was an Emmy-winning series called "My World and Welcome to It." Every Tuesday at eight in the morning I sat down at a table for a production meeting with Danny Thomas, Danny Arnold, Mel Shavelson, and Sheldon Leonard, among others. I did this for twenty-six straight weeks, and though it was called a production meeting, it was more of a discussion as to what was funny in the script, and, God forbid, what wasn't. I looked forward to those meetings like a hot fudge sundae.

After the show won an Emmy for best comedy, and William Windom won for best actor in a comedy, NBC promptly canceled it. Go figure. God knows I never added much to those comedy conversations, but everyone politely listened to anything I was brave enough to say. Imagine how I felt sitting in a land of giants.

The following year I did a short-lived series for the same company called "Make Room for Grandaddy," starring Danny Thomas. Richard Crenna was the producer. He was yet another gentleman who added to my education in comedy. Since that time he and I have worked together on a number of projects, he as director or actor. We have maintained a friendship for over thirty years, and it thrives to this day. On the phone the other day, Crenna said we have been friends for so long that one of us deserves a gold watch.

I had designed the main set for "Grandaddy" so that the walls could be moved around to accomplish shots not normally taken when shooting a multi-camera show. Crenna looked over my shoulder while I was attempting this feat, and we were both pretty excited about it. I had a model built so we could move the walls in miniature and show the weekly directors how best to make use of the set. As we got close to shooting time Danny Thomas came in to his office, and Crenna set a meeting with him so we could show him our new toy. Thomas had closed a three-week engagement in Las Vegas the night before and was understandably very tired. We walked into his office, and I plunked the model on his desk as Crenna began to explain to him the wonders of my creative genius. Thomas sat there with a foot-long cigar sticking straight out of his mouth and listened politely. After we finished our presentation he sat there a minute, and through the cigar he uttered the following: "Don't die." After a moment's silence, he continued, "Don't either of you guys play in the street. If you get hit by a truck, ain't no son of a bitch gonna understand how to work this thing." He liked it.

Why were those guys I started with so ego-free, when everyone today has assistants on the payroll just to carry their egos around in a wheelbarrow? Now there is a funny image at lunchtime at Morton's or some other power-lunch venue. The term "power lunch," by the way, was coined no more than fifteen years ago. Breakfast was breakfast, lunch was lunch, dinner was dinner, and testosterone was free. I always remember what my friend, Michael Miller says, "Sometimes you have lunch, sometimes you are lunch." That explains present-day Hollywood better than anything I've ever heard.

Celebrity. Celebrity used to mean one thing. Now it means something entirely different. The new power celebrities (God, now I'm doing it) who make more money on one picture than some countries generate in a year, are behaving as if they were kings and queens of countries. They surround themselves with bodyguards and sycophants. They hire publicists, tell them what to write, and believe it when they read it. They make themselves accessible to no one. Sure, the world is full of crazies, but if a celebrity drives down the street, parks the car, and walks into a store, no one notices. You can't ask for anonymity when traveling around surrounded by bodyguards. How rich is too rich? When you can behave like an asshole and people think you're cute, that's too rich.

I always think about this joke: Why does a dog lick his private parts? Because he can. Modern celebrities seem to want to lick themselves while you watch, and insult you if you interrupt. Now don't get me wrong. I'm not pissed off by that sort of behavior, just embarrassed. Really embarrassed.

Places I Ate

ACTUALLY, IT SHOULD BE "Places I Ate and Slept," but
I like the title so well I can't resist the music of it. People think that
show biz people only dine at Four Seasons, or 21 or the Brown
Derby (gone), or Chasen's (gone). I have indeed dined at all those
toney spots, but the most interesting places I have eaten are the
places the location manager finds for us to eat lunch, and sometimes dinner, while we're shooting.

We once had lunch in Portland in a strip joint; they remove all
clothing there. Strange place to dine. At least they could wear hair
nets. Another day in Portland, we had lunch in a chrome-plating
factory.

I have had lunch in churches, schools, and saloons, as well as
castles, forts, and the middle of the street. I have dined with
homeless people standing on the other side of a cyclone fence staring at us. (I don't recommend this. You hand your plate over the
fence and go back to work.)

In Spain they release you for lunch, and we would go to a restaurant and watch the drivers drink vast quantities of Spanish

brandy. At the end of the day, we would, if humanly possible, walk back to the hotel.

I have lunched on people's front lawns, and in fields where the ticks and chiggers dined on my ankles. I have dined in junkyards among the wreckage of Detroit's labors and people's dreams. I have been fed in hotel ballrooms and in their parking lots.

I have eaten in more parking lots than a city pigeon.

Perhaps the most interesting are the places I slept. On the Turkish island of Bozjadda, about twenty-five kilometers off the mainland from Troy, is a most beautiful fifteenth-century castle where we were doing a lot of shooting for the PBS series "Timeline." We were staying in a converted schoolhouse that was actually quite pleasant. My room, on the top floor, had a lovely little balcony. No matter where I stood in the room or on the balcony, I had the most incredible view of that castle perched on a hill overlooking the Aegean Sea. I never got tired of looking at that view—especially in the morning, when it was backlit. There was one small fishing village on the island and, in the harbor, two small restaurants. The fishermen would come back in the evening in their little one-man putt-putt boats and empty their nets at the restaurants. We would plan our evening meal around this event and wade into the middle of the flopping fish, grab what we wanted, and carry it in to one of the cooks. With much arm-waving and laughter we would explain to the chefs how we wanted them cooked. They were always accompanied by olives, French fries, the world's greatest bean soup (I have the recipe), and Turkish plums. Turkish plums are never eaten ripe, but when they are still green and about the size of apricots, with salt, they are heaven on earth. I have never found them anyplace else but in Turkey in early summer.

Of course, from the sublime of those Turkish digs, the other end of the spectrum will always be that night in Nigeria when I got bit by the mosquito.

Linda and I have made a great effort over the years to be together on our anniversaries. Those meetings have provided lots of laughs. We spent one anniversary in the bridal suite (!) of the

Hilton Inn in Salina, Kansas. The local people threw a party for us at the country club, but we were shooting at night, so I only attended long enough to dance the "Anniversary Waltz," then went back to work. Some of my gang, led by Ben Massi, our head painter, had decorated the bridal suite with crepe paper and balloons. The following morning when we got up, the balloons had lost most of their gas, and carrying the crepe paper, were an inch above our noses.

Another time on another picture, this time at the bridal suite of the Holiday Inn in Emporia, Kansas, Linda and I were cavorting around in a gaudy spa plunked down in the middle of the suite and drinking a $200 bottle of wine. Linda got very quiet for a moment, then announced, "Peter, I don't think we're in Kansas anymore."

On our twentieth anniversary, I was shooting *Under the Rainbow* on the Queen Mary in Long Beach. The company bought us the Queen Elizabeth Suite on the ship for the weekend. It was huge. The bathtubs were huge. Everything about the place was huge. The bed for the queen was king size. We had been there for one whole day when I discovered another room. Actually, it was another room and bath. It has always mystified me, as nosy as I am, how I could not have opened all the doors when we first walked into that palace on water. I truly was overwhelmed by the queenliness of it all. I probably would have made a lousy king.

One anniversary in New Orleans, I found an antebellum home on the Mississippi River that had been made into a bed-and-breakfast inn with tours during the day as well as a four-star restaurant.

I told Linda only that we were going to spend the night there. I didn't tell her, however, that I had taken the master's suite, which had a huge palm-laden living room with a fireplace and a bedroom with a four-poster bed and a fireplace. It also had a nursery complete with cradle I didn't plan to use, and a large front porch without a fireplace. I also didn't tell her about the dining arrangements.

Instead of eating in the restaurant, I had them hire us another waiter to serve us in our suite. I prearranged the menu with the

Linda still gives me big ice cream cones.

chef, and it ran to five courses. I put on a suit and Linda got all dressed up thinking we were going to the dining room. We walked across the lawn to the restaurant and had a glass of champagne. Then I gave the chef a signal, and dragged Linda back to the suite where the waiter had set the most exquisite table for us.

He served with white-glove silence and slipped into the hall to await my ringing a bell for the next course. When it came time for dessert, the chef came in and flambéd bananas Foster for us.

I also neglected to tell Linda that we had to be out of the room by nine in the morning or we would become part of the tour.

We were preparing to shoot in another bed-and-breakfast for a miniseries called "Broken Commandments." We were going to shoot in a unique round bedroom in the inn, and the night before, Linda and I took it over. We were rudely awakened the next morning by the assistant director pounding on the door and yelling for us to get the hell out of there. The actors were ready to come in and shoot. To some people, that could have been embarrassing.

We did the same thing in Montreal. I had found this most elegant inn about to open in Old Town, and I wanted to shoot there for yet another miniseries, "Zoya." Although the restaurant had been open for some time, the inn had not yet seen its first customer. Linda flew in for another yearly event, and I made arrangements for them to open early just for us. We had an elegant weekend with the help of a very discreet butler who sort of magically appeared and disappeared, as well as an English bulldog named Charles who snorted about and gave amorous attention to my leg. I figured that was how the idle rich lived.

I once hired a limousine to drive us from my apartment in Albuquerque to the best restaurant in Santa Fe and back again. Over the years I have found that no matter where you are, it is relatively easy to create a memorable moment if your heart is really in it. That could be one of the reasons we have been happily married for almost forty-five years. Having Linda for a wife makes it very easy for my heart to be in it.

Inserts

Dullness is the coming of age of seriousness.
—*Oscar Wilde*

THE FOLLOWING is a compendium of stories and moments that have found a place in my heart and will not leave. They are in no particular order, and they do not necessarily relate to one another.

From time to time other people's stories come my way that deserve to be passed on. My friend Charles Rosen, also a production designer, tells this one: He was hired to design the movie *Ordinary People*, and the studio had him fly back to Columbus, Ohio, to meet with the director, Robert Redford. Redford was starring in the film *Brubaker*, which was being shot at the Ohio State Penitentiary. Rosen got to the prison in his rental car about a half-hour before wrap, and Redford said, "When we wrap, if you'll take me home we'll talk about the script and have a glass of wine."

At this point, Chuck tells the story of telling the story to his wife, Marygrace. "So, honey, I drove Bob to this wonderful romantic cottage that the studio had rented for him out in the woods. As we approached the cottage it began to rain. I parked, and we ran laughing through the rain. Inside, the cottage was really romantic. Hardwood floors and a big stone fireplace, and out every window was a view of rain-soaked woods. Bob immediately built a roaring fire, then opened a bottle of wine. He got a couple of steaks from the 'fridge, showed 'em to me, and put them under the broiler, all the time making small talk and keeping the moment light.

"So, there we were, honey, sitting at opposite ends of the couch, drinking wine in front of the fire, and it dawned on me at that moment, sitting there with Robert Redford, every woman in the world would love to be where I was, and…"

"Never mind that!" Marygrace broke in. "Did you fuck him?"

Ward Preston, another production designer, was on location in Emporia, Kansas, doing a Hallmark Hall of Fame movie, *Mary White*. He was driving with his head painter, Chuck Clark, to a set they were constructing out in the middle of nowhere. Chuck had a touch of stomach flu and suddenly had need of a restroom. Nothing. No gas station, no farmhouse, no such thing as a restroom. Nothing. As the poor fellow was becoming increasingly desperate, they came upon an abandoned farmhouse with an out-house in the back. Ward slammed on the brakes, and Chuck bolted. The door of the outhouse fell off the hinges as he flew in.

Time passed and out came the painter looking around in con-fusion. "Now what's wrong?" Ward yelled in exasperation.

"I'm looking for a long stick."

"What the hell for?"

"My jacket fell down the other hole in the outhouse."

"Good God, man, forget the jacket. I'll buy you a new one when I get back to town."

"I can't," cried the painter, "my lunch is in the pocket."

Thinking about Emporia, Kansas, reminds me of the time I was there doing a mini-series called "Broken Commandments." It was a true story that had taken place in Emporia some four short years before we arrived to do the film. It was the tale of a local minister who was having an affair with one of his parishioners. He and his lady-friend up and killed his wife and her husband, which is decidedly not a ministerly thing to do. By the time we arrived on the scene, they were both doing big time in the Kansas State Peni-tentiary. We wanted to tell their story using the same locations where the actual events had taken place.

Now, it is said that Emporia, Kansas, is the buckle of the Bible belt. There are fifty-some churches there, and not one of them wanted us to tell this story. The rest of the city was all for it. Like they say in Hollywood, "We don't care what you say about us, as long as you spell our names right." The churches, however, had another point of view, and we needed to shoot in a church. I arranged meetings at every church that filled my shooting needs and sat through a number of meetings with board members, only to be insulted. The final insult came one night at a board meeting in a beautiful old Baptist church.

Sitting across from me at the table was an old Kansas farmer dressed in bib overalls. After I made my presentation, I sat back to await the decision. I knew what was coming.

The old man spoke: "A while back I had a couple calves. Had 'em out on the back forty. Grass was pretty high back there and I lost track of 'em for a bit. By and by I saw a bunch of buzzards circlin' back in the corner. That's what I think of you, just a bunch of circlin' buzzards."

I slammed my hand down on the table and declared the meeting adjourned. We shot the church sequences in Lawrence, Kansas.

Okay, That's a Wrap

---

*The best career advice given to the young is
"Find out what you like doing best, and get
someone to pay you for doing it."*
　　　　　　　　—*Katherine Whitehorn*

THIRTY-FOUR THOUSAND FEET. My ass again in
leather. I'm returning from yet another adventure. I just finished
another movie for Lifetime Television, *Blue Valley Songbird.* We
shot it in Nashville, Tennessee, and it starred Dolly Parton. The
script was based on a song she wrote by the same title. It had lots
of music, and Dolly did it proud.

Now, there is some kind of lady. Dolly Parton is as unique an
individual as you will ever find anyplace. Not for her obvious at-
tributes, which are…um…well, obvious. Rather, for what is not so
obvious. First of all, she has an IQ at least twenty points higher
than anyone thinks it is. She is a consummate professional at all
times. She is always on time and prepared to do her job. She
knows her lines, helps the other actors with theirs, and spends the
day in good humor. She ends her day thanking us all for doing a
good job (Dolly was also the executive producer), and she "hangs
out" on the set with the guys, like she couldn't imagine being anywhere else. There was not one person on the company, male or fe-
male, who wasn't in love with her. I was prepared to fall in love
with Dolly just from the way people who had worked with her

"Don't move, there's a bee on your blouse."

talked about her. She, however, made it very easy. The movie was directed by my playmate, Richard Colla, so that made it doubly fun. If movies could be made like this all the time, I would never retire. From the day I stepped off the plane in Nashville to today, when Richard and I stepped back on, I have had what can only be described as the most fun you can have with your pants on. He's sitting next to me with his ass in leather and a reasonably good glass of cognac in hand.

Life does not suck. You can quote me.